MW00667250

Dear Colleagues,

As middle school and high school band directors, we often need an alternative fingering, a trill fingering, or a fingering for a note in an extreme range. In addition, we find it difficult to locate information concerning percussion instrument ranges, the location of middle C on the keyboard percussion instruments, and a clear, yet thorough, presentation of the standard snare drum rudiments in a single source.

Likewise, our students are in the same situation. As our students grow into their musical maturity, they often need a quick, reliable reference for fingerings, ranges, and ornamentation. Percussionists are required to perform on instruments that are provided at a concert or audition site. Having a reference of percussion instrument ranges has helped our percussionists to adapt to these different settings.

This reference guide provides you with the following information:

- Advanced range fingering chart (including alternate fingerings) for all wind instruments

- Trill chart and key diagram for all woodwind instruments

- Harmonic series indicating pitch tendencies for all brass instruments

- Ornamentation guide (trills, turns, mordents, grace notes) for brass

- Ranges for all keyboard percussion instruments

- Major scale & arpeggio diagrams for keyboard percussion

- Timpani sizes and ranges

- All 40 standard drum rudiments

We hope you and your students find this guide to be a useful reference tool.

Richard Williams   Jeff King

Flute Key Diagram

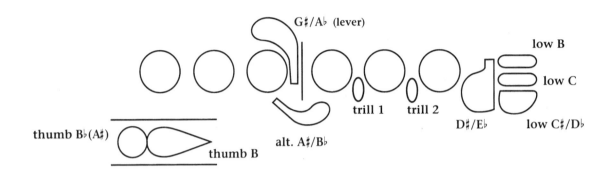

WARNING!

It is **illegal** to photocopy or reproduce the Flute Key Diagram and Fingering Charts. Individual Flute Key Diagram and Fingering Charts are available for purchase from your favorite music dealer for use with your students. Please refer to the back cover of this manual for further information.

Individual Flute Key Diagram and Fingering Charts
Kjos Edition Number - W33FL

kjos *Neil A. Kjos Music Company*

Flute Fingering Chart

The thumb B-flat key may be used on all fingerings except 3rd line B-natural, F-sharp/G-flat, and B-natural above the staff.

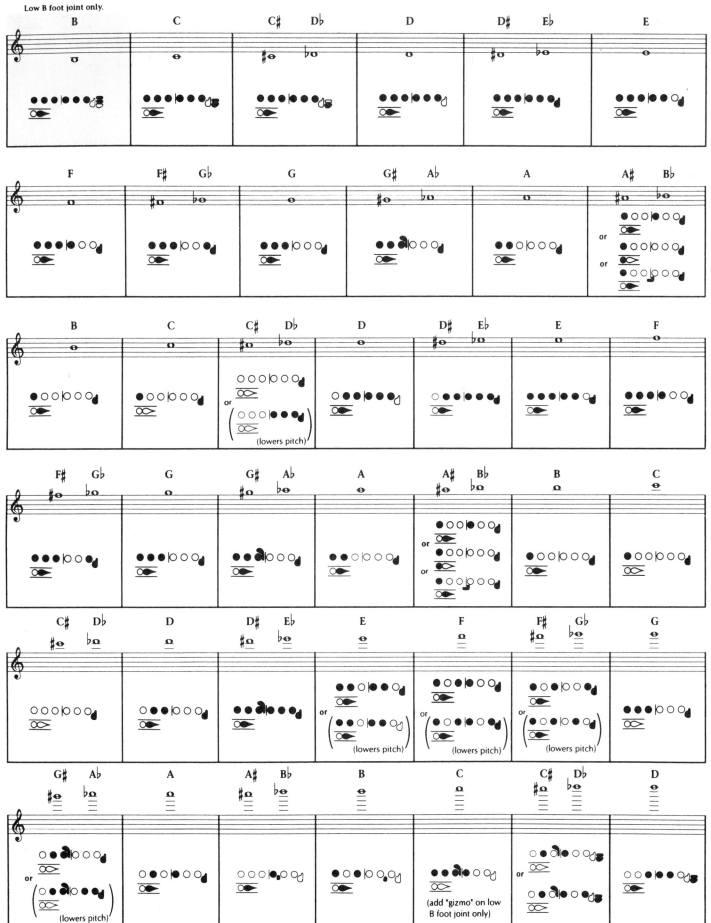

(When more than one fingering is shown, the first is the most common.)

It is **illegal** to photocopy or reproduce this Flute Fingering Chart.

W33F

Flute Trill Fingering Chart

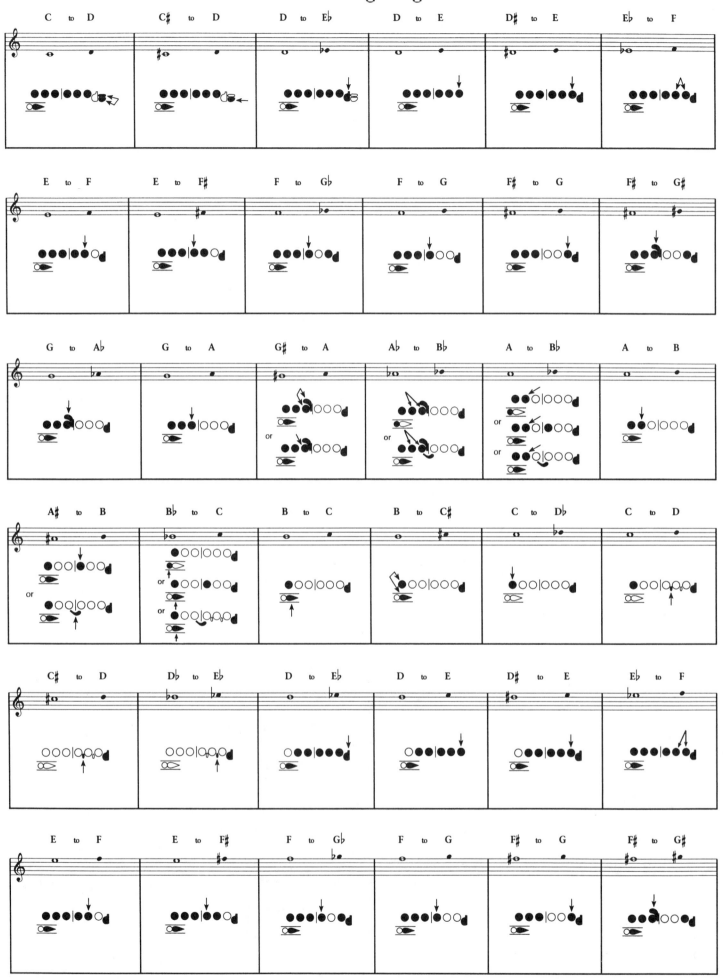

(The arrow(s) indicate the key(s) to be trilled.)

It is **illegal** to photocopy or reproduce this Flute Trill Fingering Chart.

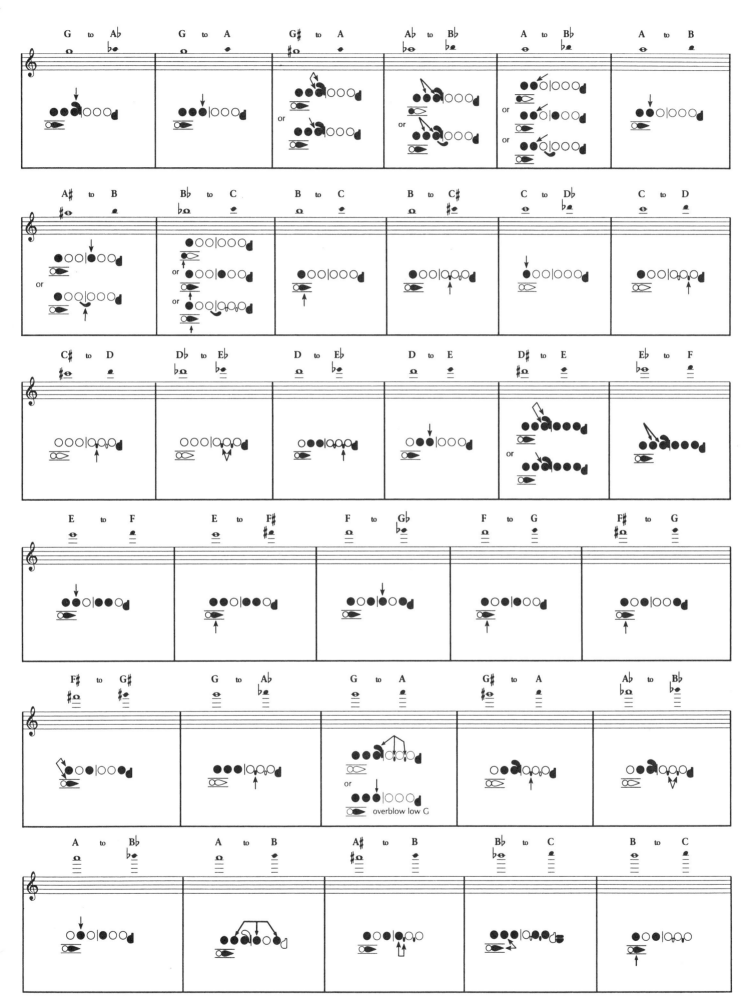

(When more than one fingering is shown, the first is the most common.)

It is **illegal** to photocopy or reproduce this Flute Trill Fingering Chart.

W33F

Oboe Key Diagram

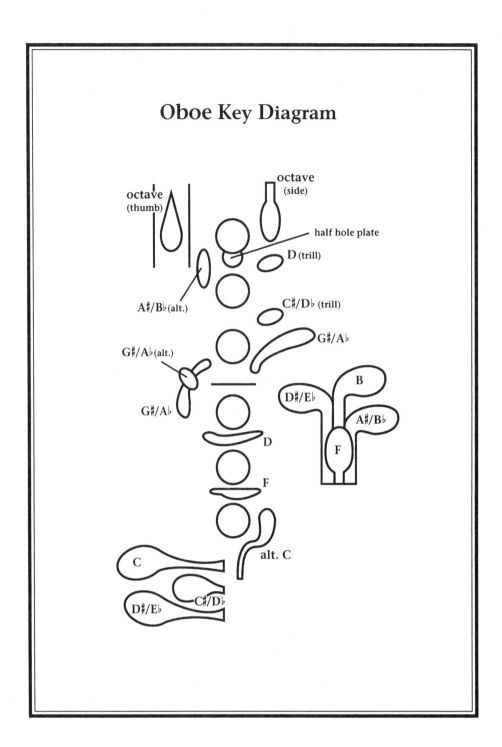

WARNING!

It is **illegal** to photocopy or reproduce the Oboe Key Diagram and Fingering Charts. Individual Oboe Key Diagram and Fingering Charts are available for purchase from your favorite music dealer for use with your students. Please refer to the back cover of this manual for further information.

Individual Oboe Key Diagram and Fingering Charts
Kjos Edition Number - W33OB

ΚʄOS *Neil A. Kjos Music Company*

Oboe Fingering Chart

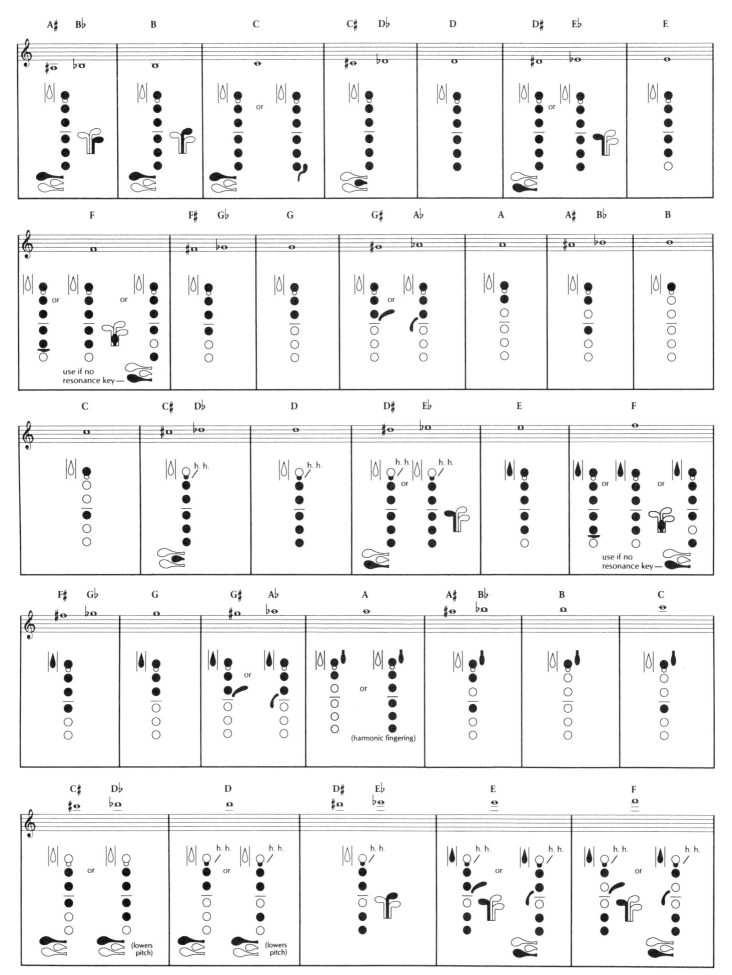

(When more than one fingering is shown, the first is the most common.)

It is **illegal** to photocopy or reproduce this Oboe Fingering Chart.

Oboe Trill Fingering Chart

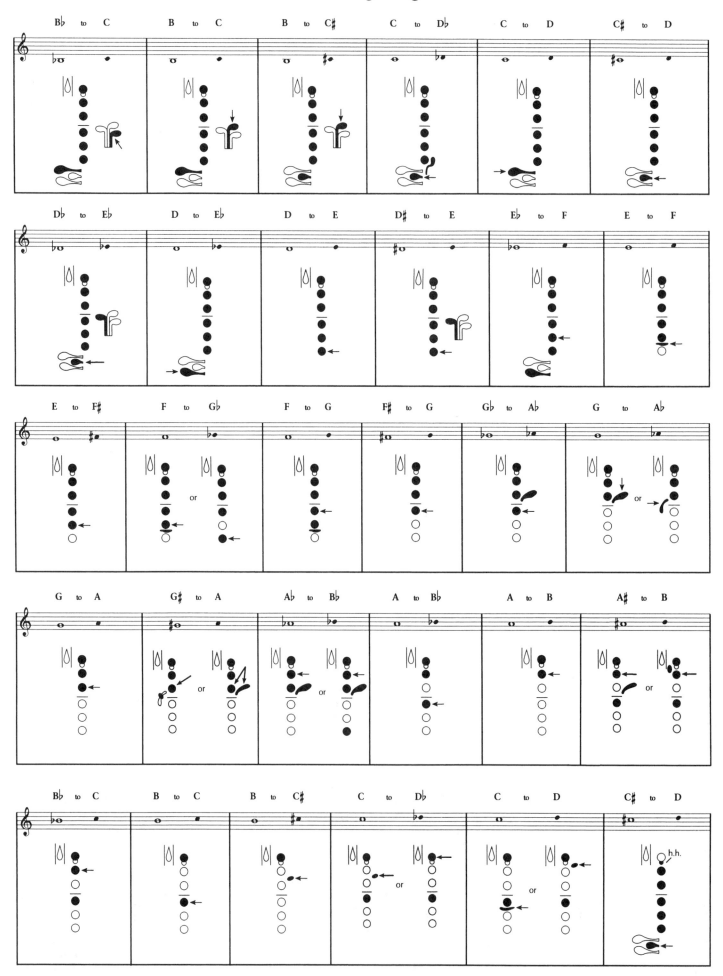

(The arrow(s) indicate the key(s) to be trilled.)

It is **illegal** to photocopy or reproduce this Oboe Trill Fingering Chart.

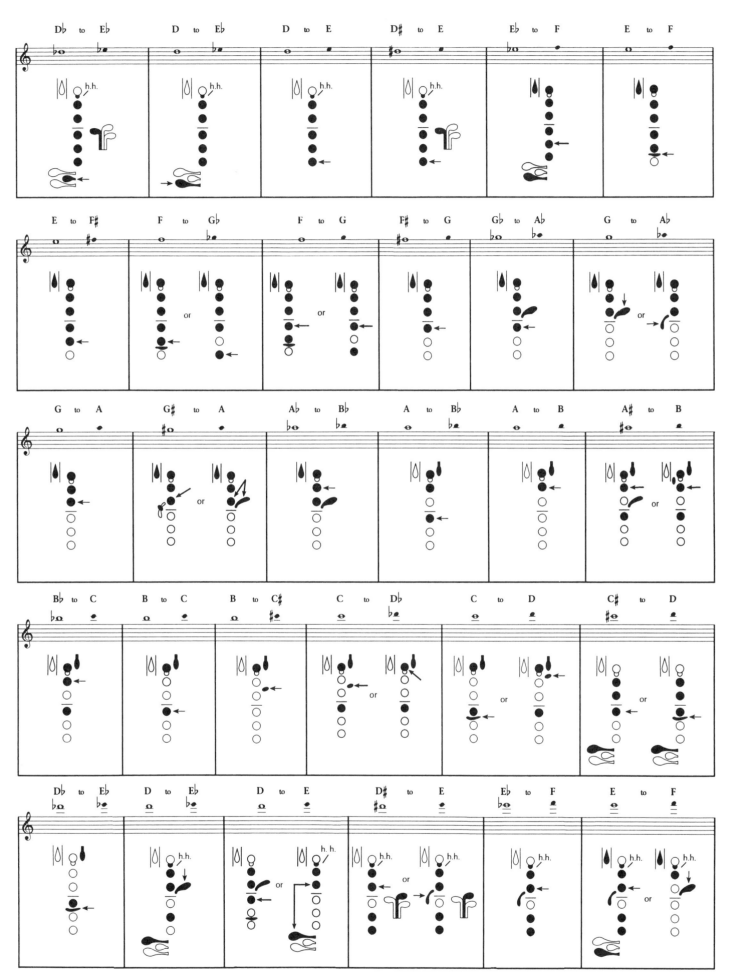

(When more than one fingering is shown, the first is the most common.)

It is **illegal** to photocopy or reproduce this Oboe Trill Fingering Chart.

Bassoon Key Diagram

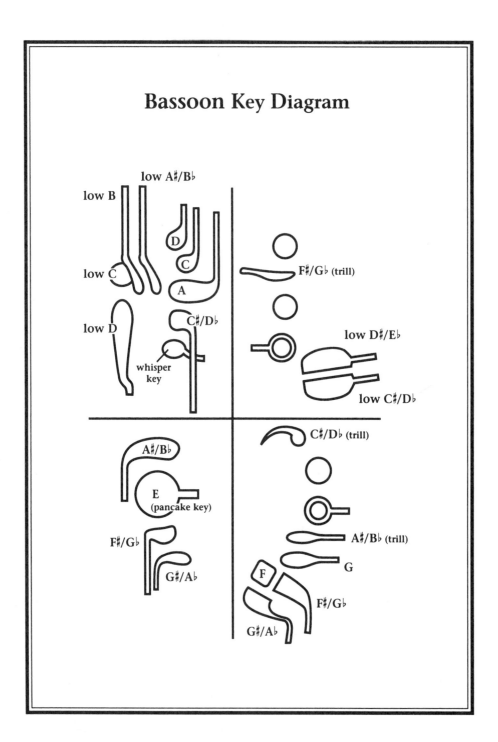

WARNING!

It is **illegal** to photocopy or reproduce the Bassoon Key Diagram and Fingering Charts. Individual Bassoon Key Diagram and Fingering Charts are available for purchase from your favorite music dealer for use with your students. Please refer to the back cover of this manual for further information.

Individual Bassoon Key Diagram and Fingering Charts
Kjos Edition Number - W33BN

kjos *Neil A. Kjos Music Company*

Bassoon Fingering Chart

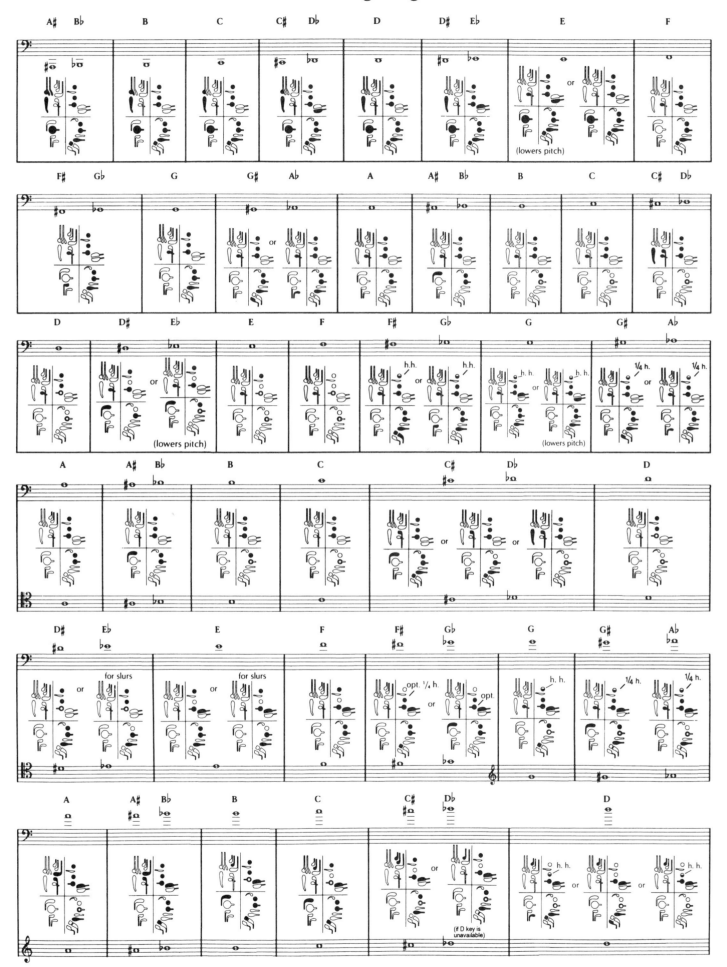

(When more than one fingering is shown, the first is the most common.)

It is **illegal** to photocopy or reproduce this Bassoon Fingering Chart.

Bassoon Trill Fingering Chart

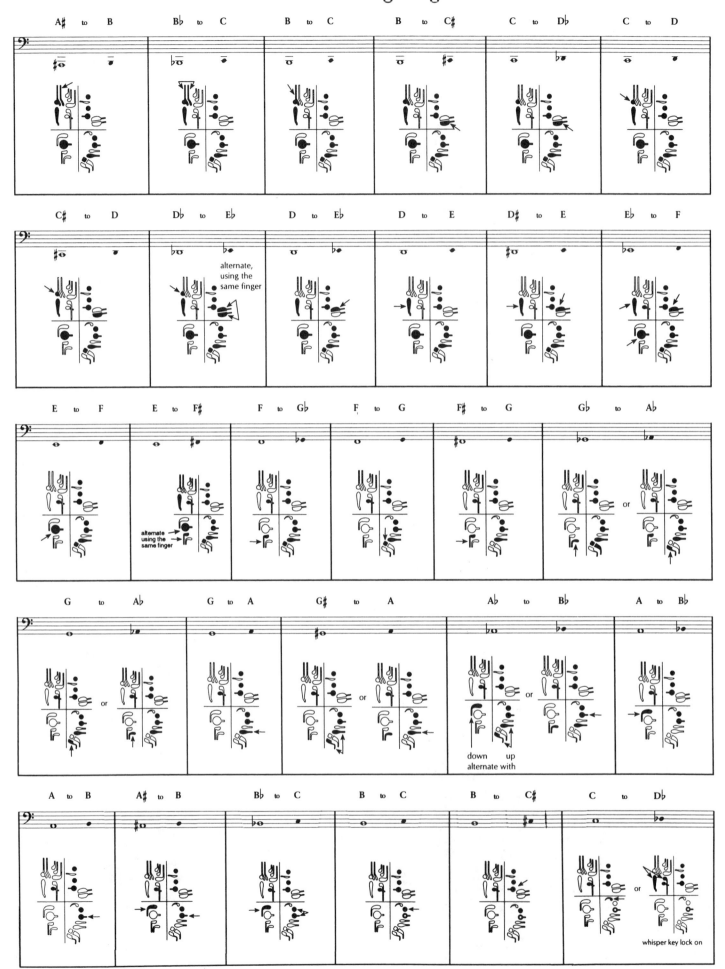

(The arrow(s) indicate the key(s) to be trilled.)

It is **illegal** to photocopy or reproduce this Bassoon Trill Fingering Chart.

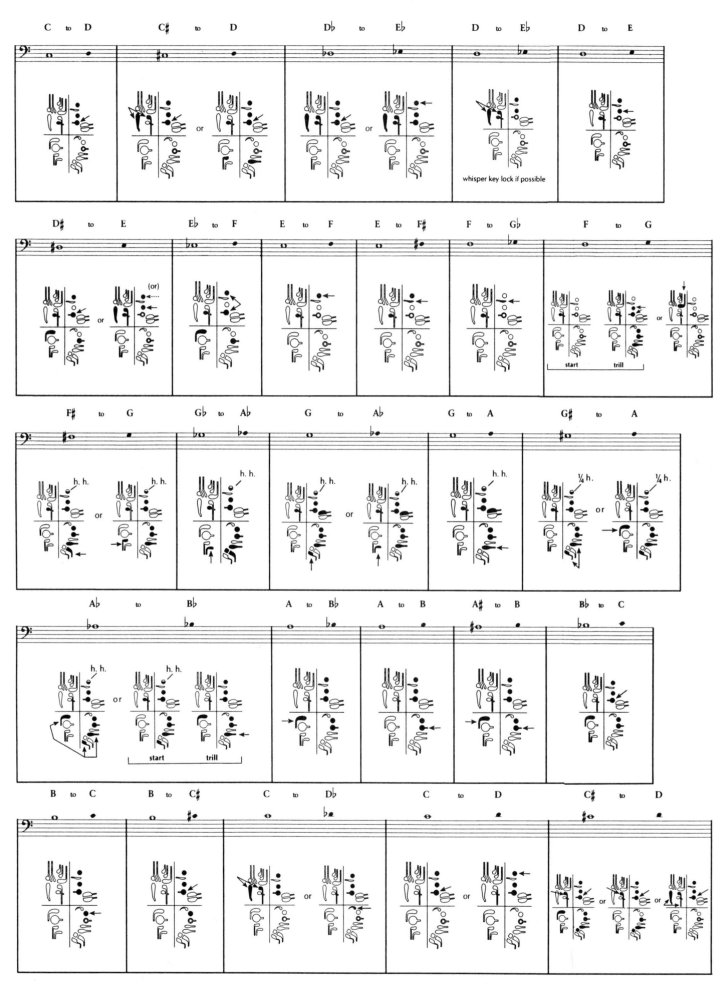

(When more than one fingering is shown, the first is the most common.)

It is **illegal** to photocopy or reproduce this Bassoon Trill Fingering Chart.

14

Bassoon Trill Fingering Chart (Cont.)

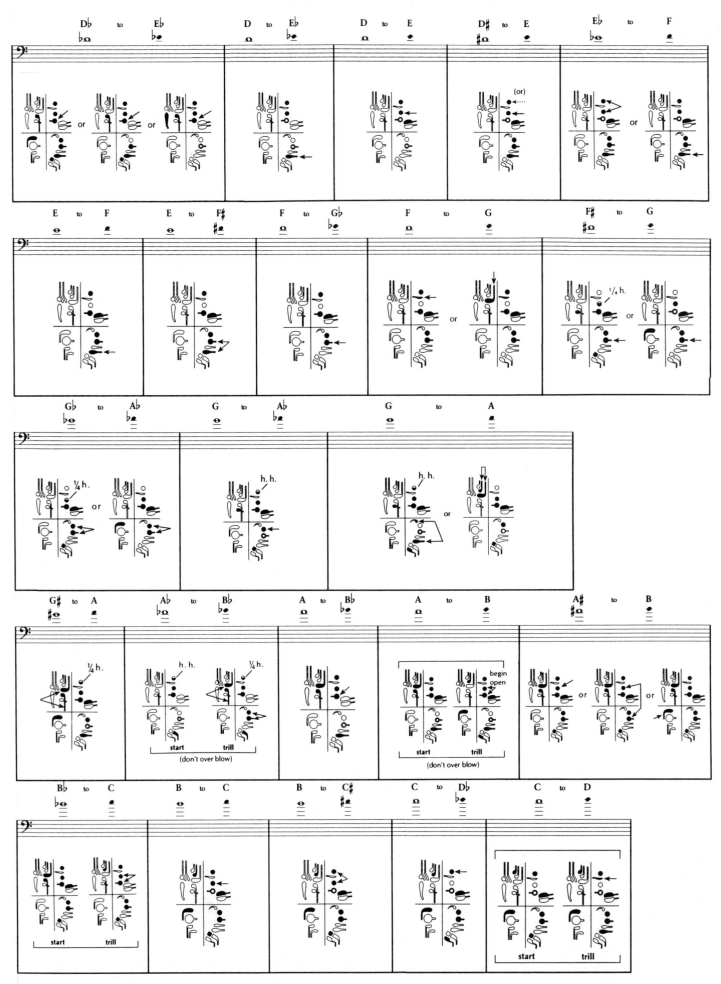

(The arrow(s) indicate the key(s) to be trilled.)

It is **illegal** to photocopy or reproduce this Bassoon Trill Fingering Chart.

Special Bassoon Fingerings & Techniques

Like all woodwind instruments, the bassoon has a "break" between the first and second register. To negotiate this register change smoothly, the player must be proficient in half-hole technique. The transitional notes that require a half-hole fingering are:

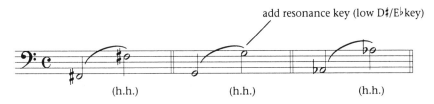

To determine the correct size of the half-hole, practice the slurs below. Start in the low octave and *roll* the first finger downward to the half-hole position. When the low note jumps to the upper octave, the size of the half-hole is correct. ***Always roll the finger to create the half-hole - never pick it up and place it in position.***

add resonance key (low D♯/E♭ key)

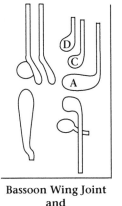

Bassoon Wing Joint and Flick/Speaker Keys

Flicking is a technique used to facilitate certain slurs. The keys used for flicking are located on the wing joint; they are the high A, C, and D keys. Note that the high D key is not available on all bassoons. These keys are also used to facilitate attacks - or getting certain notes to "speak" cleanly with resonance.

"Flicking" is accomplished with the left thumb. At the exact moment that the fingers depress the slurred, or tongued note that needs to be flicked, the left thumb lightly opens the appropriate flick key for an instant (do not fully depress the flick key).

Use the indicated flick keys when slurring from any note in this range: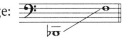

to these notes:

flick high A   flick high C   flick high D (if available)

Remember that the flick keys can also improve the tone quality and response of these notes when they are articulated.

Octave and Flick exercises - practice slowly:

Octave Slurs

flick A key   flick C key   flick C key   flick C key   flick C key / flick D key (if available)

Flick Etude (slurs with fingering changes)

"Speaker-Key" Etude (use flick keys for clear attacks)

It is **illegal** to photocopy or reproduce this Special Bassoon Fingerings and Techniques page.

W33F

Clarinet Key Diagram

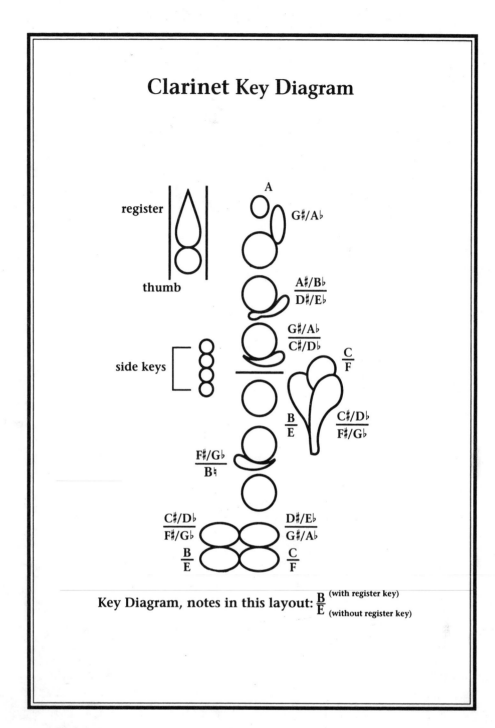

Key Diagram, notes in this layout: $\frac{B}{E}$ (with register key) / (without register key)

WARNING!

It is **illegal** to photocopy or reproduce the Clarinet Key Diagram and Fingering Charts. Individual Clarinet Key Diagram and Fingering Charts are available for purchase from your favorite music dealer for use with your students. Please refer to the back cover of this manual for further information.

Individual Clarinet Key Diagram and Fingering Charts
Kjos Edition Number - W33CL

kjos *Neil A. Kjos Music Company*

Clarinet Fingering Chart

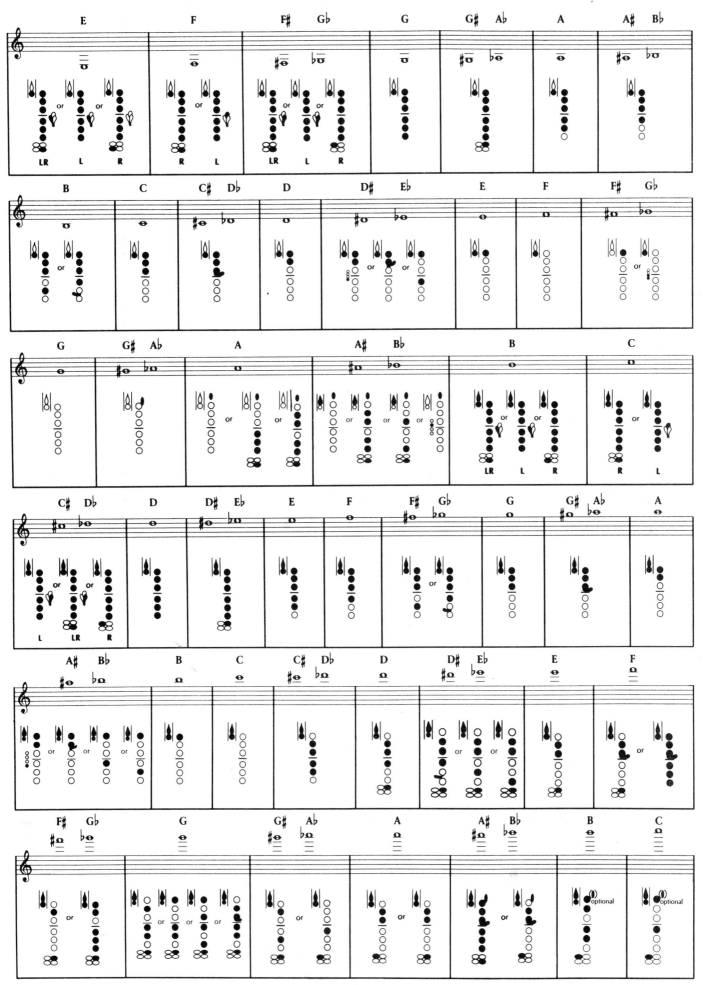

(When more than one fingering is shown, the first is the most common.)

It is **illegal** to photocopy or reproduce this Clarinet Fingering Chart.

18

Clarinet Trill Fingering Chart

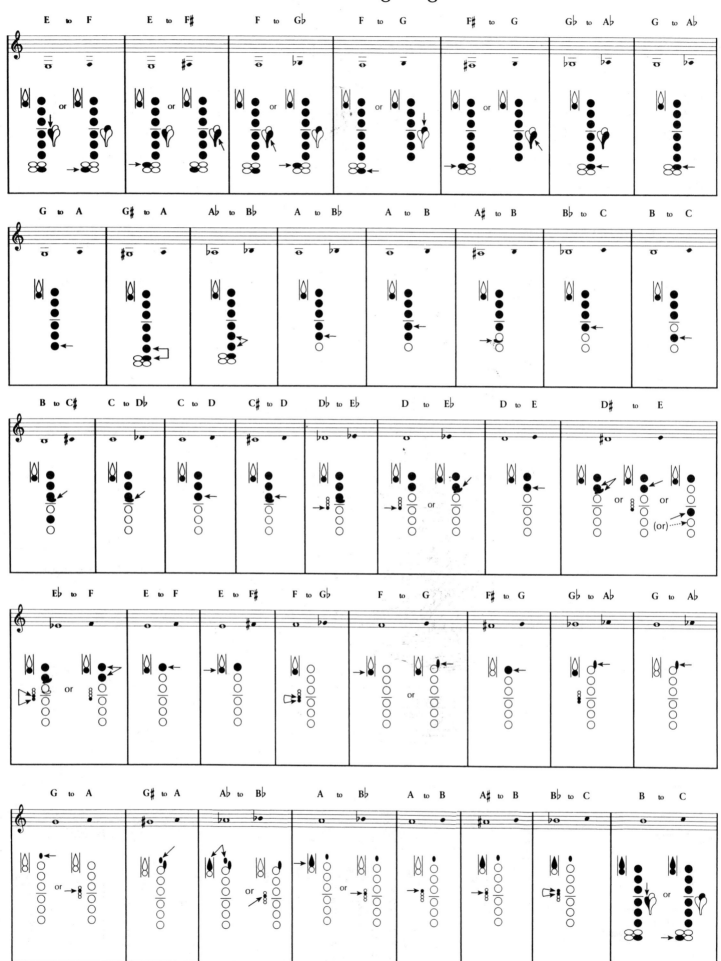

(The arrow(s) indicate the key(s) to be trilled.)

It is **illegal** to photocopy or reproduce this Clarinet Trill Fingering Chart.

W33F

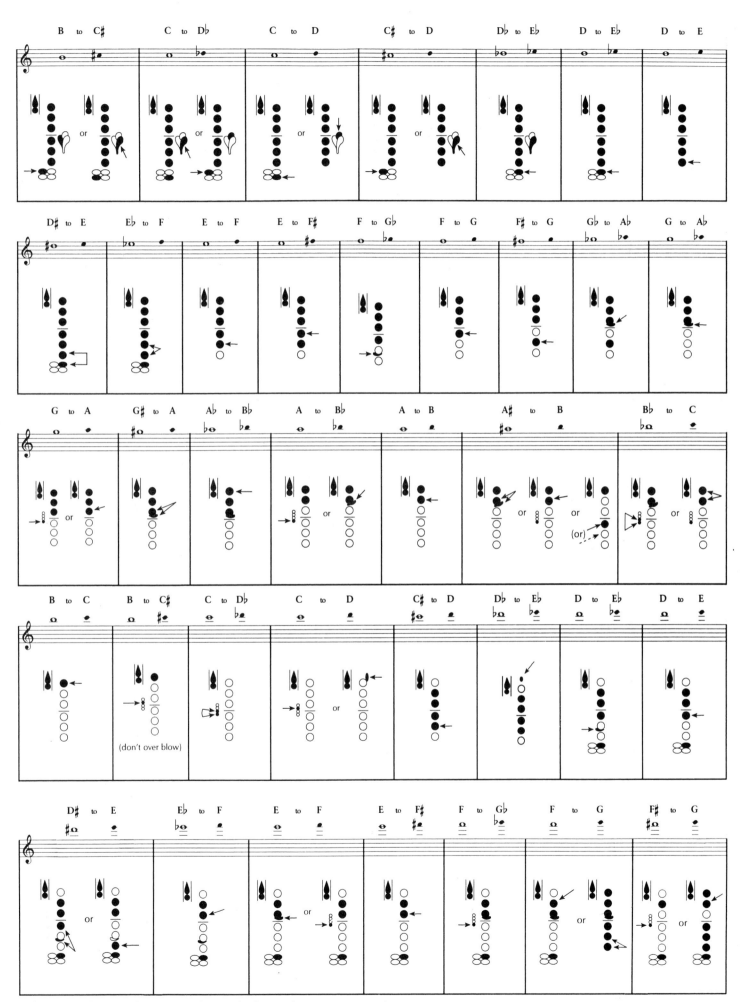

(When more than one fingering is shown, the first is the most common.)

It is **illegal** to photocopy or reproduce this Clarinet Trill Fingering Chart.

Bass Clarinet
Alto Clarinet/Contralto Clarinet
Key Diagram

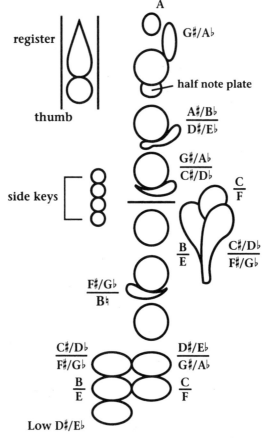

Key Diagram, notes in this layout: $\frac{B}{E}$ (with register key) (without register key)

WARNING!

It is **illegal** to photocopy or reproduce the Bass Clarinet/Alto Clarinet/Contralto Clarinet Key Diagram and Fingering Charts. Individual Bass Clarinet/Alto Clarinet/Contralto Clarinet Key Diagram and Fingering Charts are available for purchase from your favorite music dealer for use with your students. Please refer to the back cover of this manual for further information.

Individual Bass Clarinet/Alto Clarinet/Contralto Clarinet
Key Diagram and Fingering Charts
Kjos Edition Number - W33CLB

kjos *Neil A. Kjos Music Company*

Bass Clarinet/Alto Clarinet/Contralto Clarinet Fingering Chart

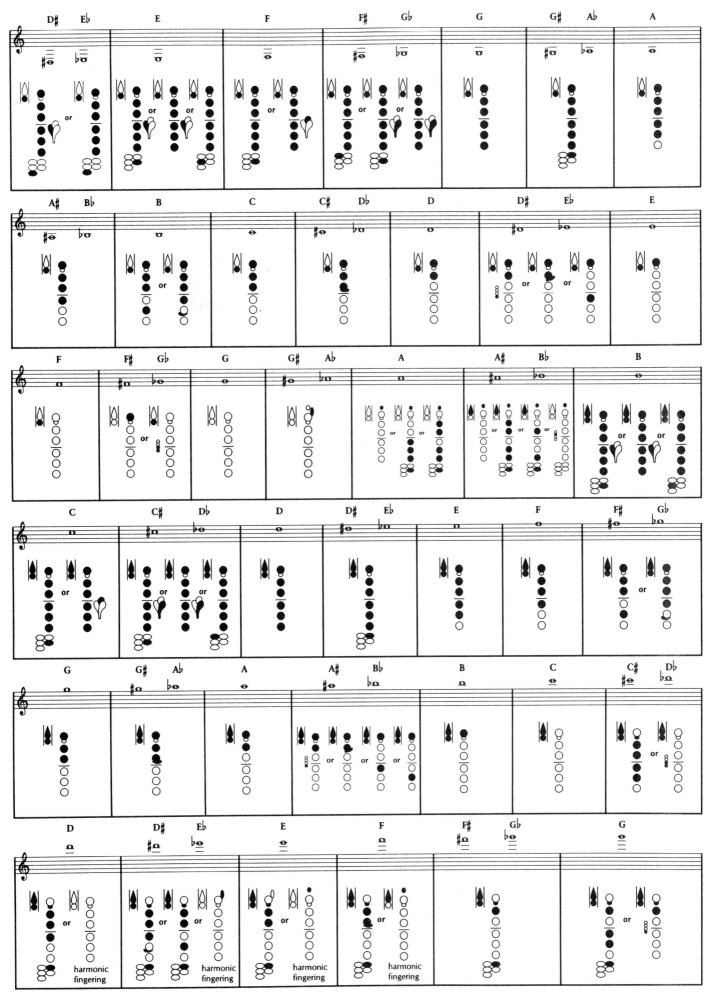

(When more than one fingering is shown, the first is the most common.)

It is **illegal** to photocopy or reproduce this Bass Clarinet/Alto Clarinet/Contralto Clarinet Fingering Chart.

Bass Clarinet/Alto Clarinet/Contralto Clarinet Trill Fingering Chart

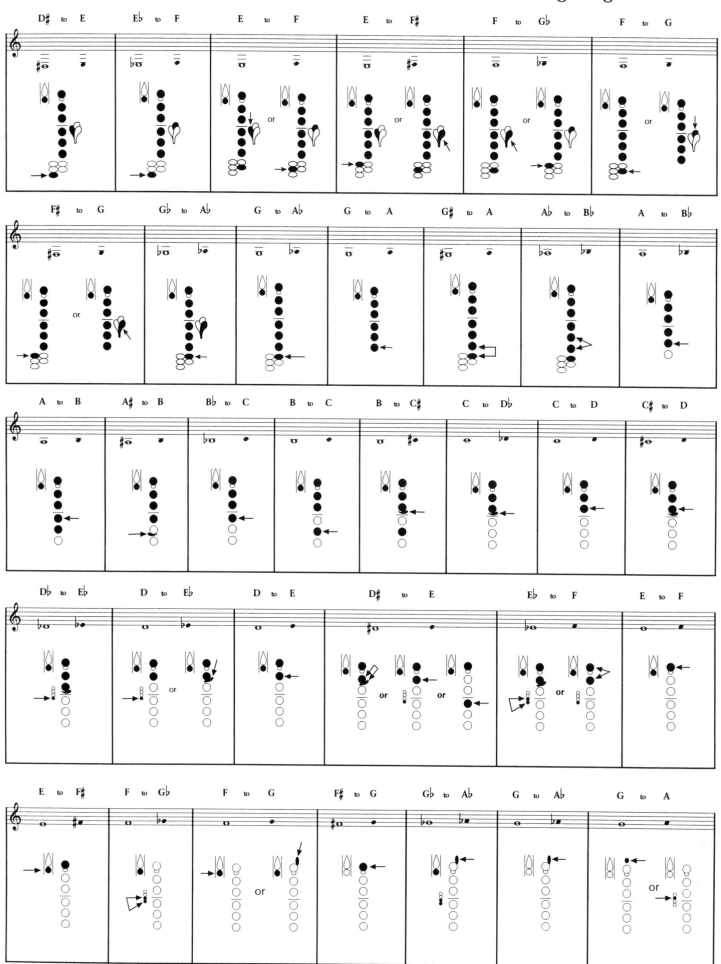

(The arrow(s) indicate the key(s) to be trilled.)

It is **illegal** to photocopy or reproduce this Bass Clarinet/Alto Clarinet/Contralto Clarinet Trill Fingering Chart.
W33F

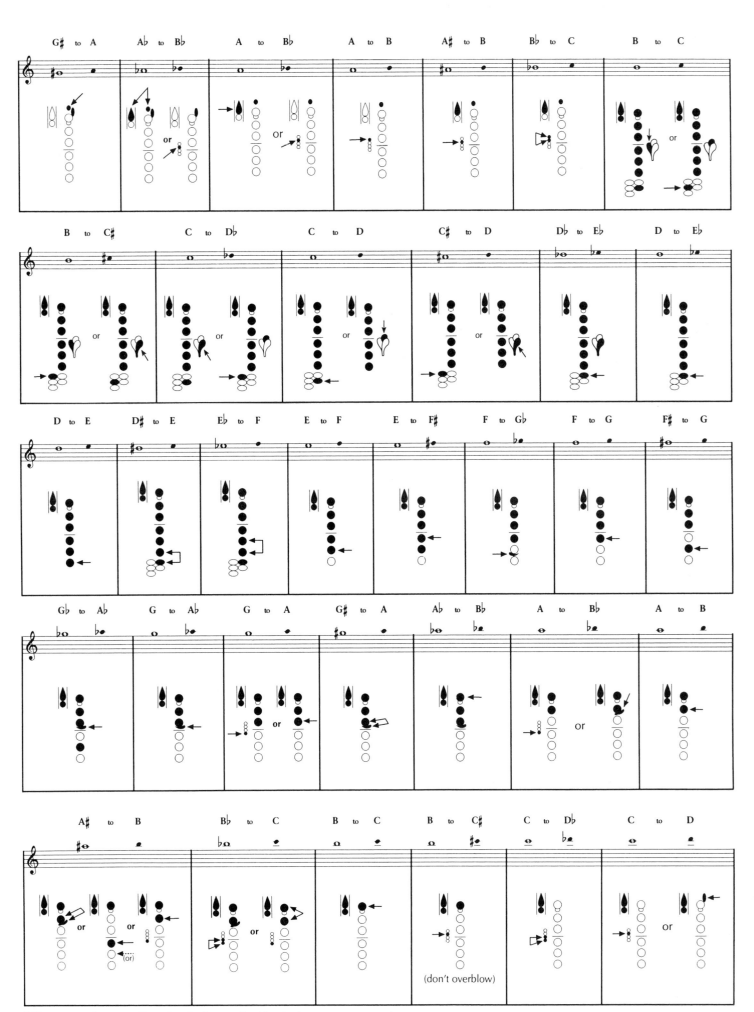

(When more than one fingering is shown, the first is the most common.)

It is **illegal** to photocopy or reproduce this Bass Clarinet/Alto Clarinet/Contralto Clarinet Trill Fingering Chart.

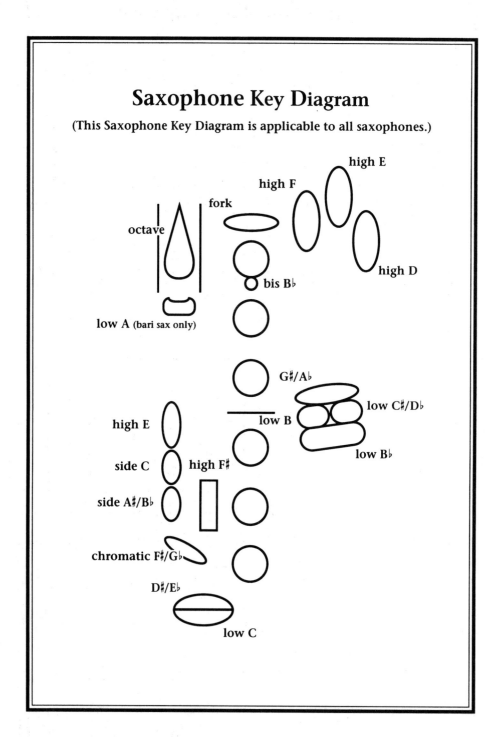

Saxophone Key Diagram

(This Saxophone Key Diagram is applicable to all saxophones.)

high E

high F

fork

octave

bis B♭

high D

low A (bari sax only)

G♯/A♭

low C♯/D♭

high E

low B

low B♭

side C

high F♯

side A♯/B♭

chromatic F♯/G♭

D♯/E♭

low C

WARNING!

It is **illegal** to photocopy or reproduce the Saxophone Key Diagram and Fingering Charts. Individual Saxophone Key Diagram and Fingering Charts are available for purchase from your favorite music dealer for use with your students. Please refer to the back cover of this manual for further information.

Individual Saxophone Key Diagram and Fingering Charts
Kjos Edition Numbers: Alto Saxophone - W33XE, Tenor Saxophone - W33XB
Baritone Saxophone - W33XR

kjos *Neil A. Kjos Music Company*

Alto Saxophone Fingering Chart

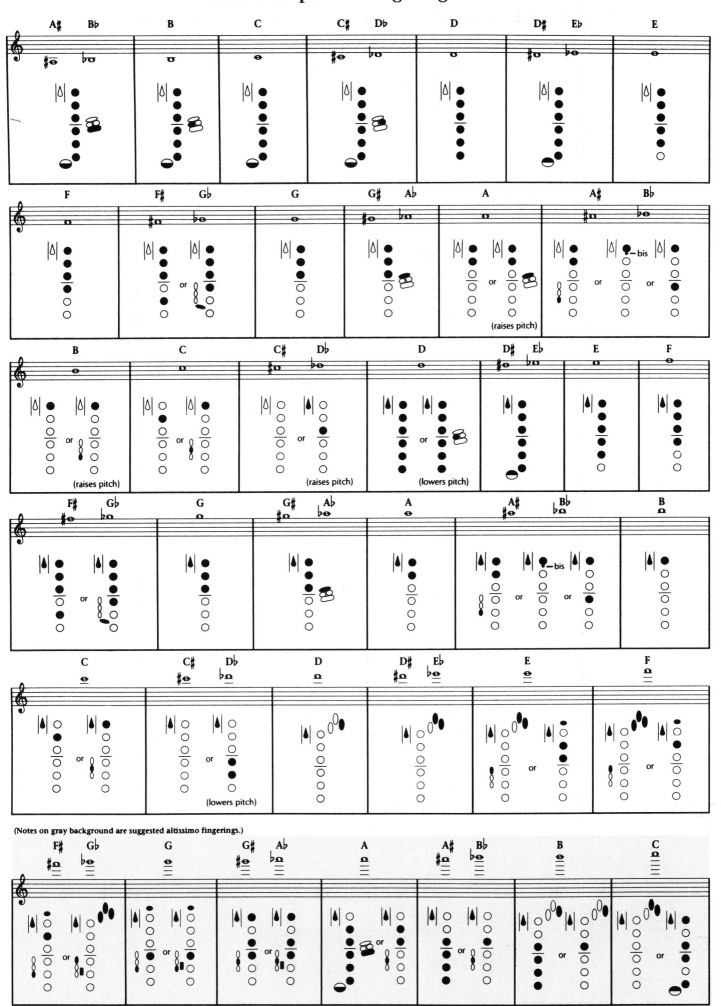

(Notes on gray background are suggested altissimo fingerings.)

(When more than one fingering is shown, the first is the most common.)

It is **illegal** to photocopy or reproduce this Alto Saxophone Fingering Chart.

W33F

Tenor Saxophone Fingering Chart

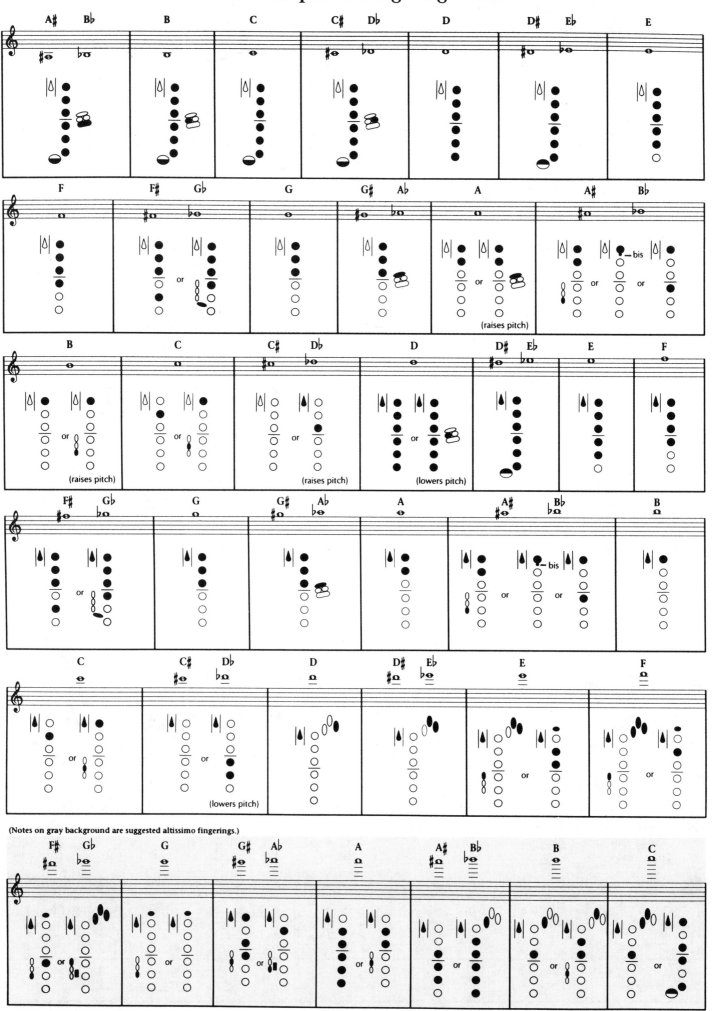

(Notes on gray background are suggested altissimo fingerings.)

(When more than one fingering is shown, the first is the most common.)

It is **illegal** to photocopy or reproduce this Tenor Saxophone Fingering Chart.

Baritone Saxophone Fingering Chart

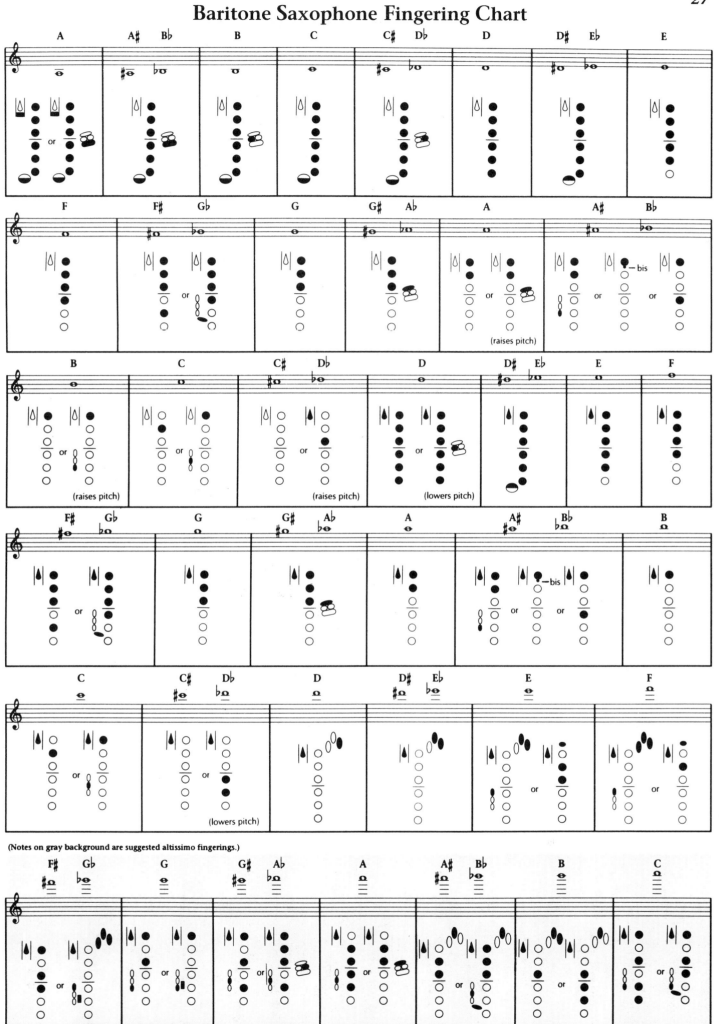

(Notes on gray background are suggested altissimo fingerings.)

(When more than one fingering is shown, the first is the most common.)

It is **illegal** to photocopy or reproduce this Baritone Saxophone Fingering Chart.

W33F

Saxophone Trill Fingering Chart
(This chart is applicable to all saxophones.)

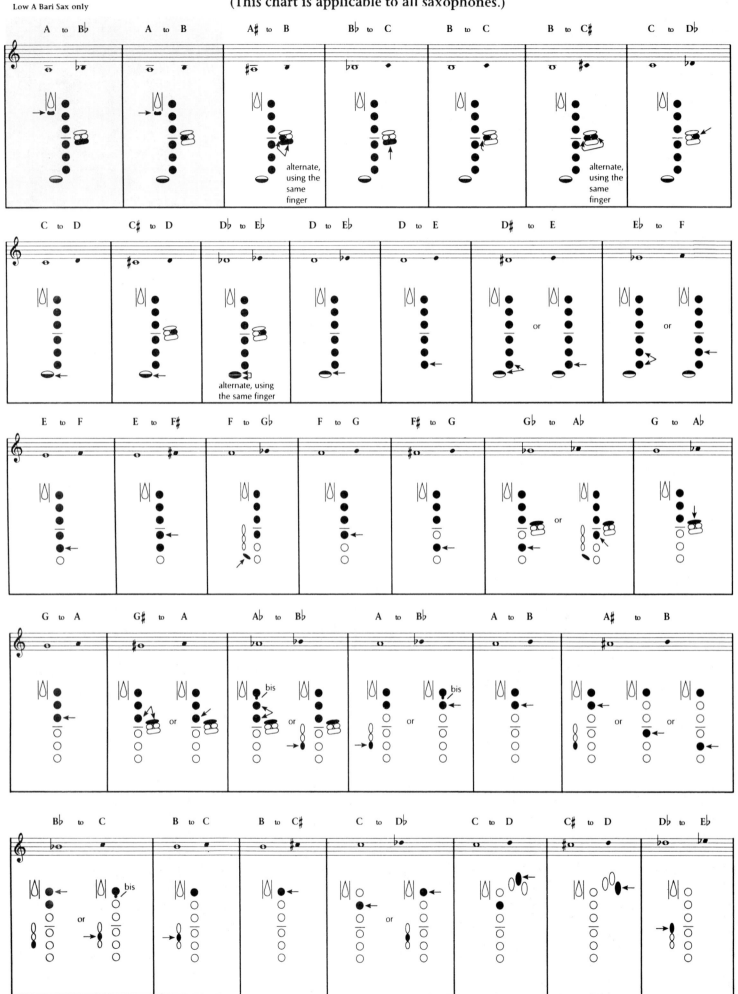

(The arrow(s) indicate the key(s) to be trilled.)

It is **illegal** to photocopy or reproduce this Saxophone Trill Fingering Chart.

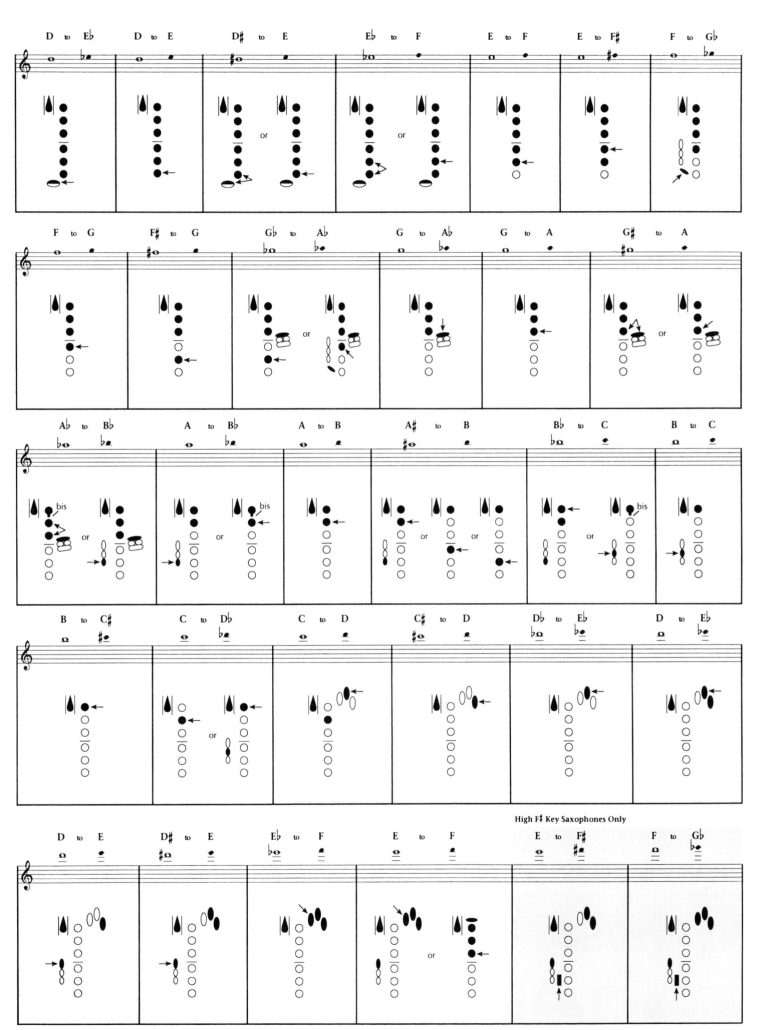

(When more than one fingering is shown, the first is the most common.)

It is **illegal** to photocopy or reproduce this Saxophone Trill Fingering Chart.

Trumpet/Cornet Harmonic Series

The fundamental pitch of the trumpet/cornet is determined by the length of the tube. Its characteristic tone quality is determined not only by the size of the opening in the tube, but also the amount of conical tubing or flare.

Regardless of the length of tubing, a natural overtone series is produced when the air inside the tube is activated through the vibration of the lips. By changing the tension of the lips and air speed, the performer can move higher and lower within the harmonic series, without changing valves. Although the harmonic series is (in theory) endless, the chart below begins with the fundamental and continues through the 10th partial. *However, different brands of instruments and mouthpieces may produce varying results.*

The 7th harmonic (partial) is so flat that it is unusable in the series (note the triangular shape of the note head). The 5th partial is noticeably flat while the 3rd and 6th harmonics are slightly sharp.

Although the first partial (fundamental) is included on this chart, the small bore of the trumpet/cornet does not allow these notes to be played with a characteristic tone.

WARNING! It is **illegal** to photocopy or reproduce the Trumpet Harmonic Series and Fingering Chart. Individual Trumpet Fingering Charts are available for purchase from your favorite music dealer for use with your students. Please refer to the back cover of this manual for further information.

Individual Trumpet Fingering Charts: Kjos Edition Number - W33TP

Trumpet Fingering Chart

(Notes on gray background are pedal tones – younger players should use 1 2 3 for all pedal tones.)

C	C♯ D♭	D	D♯ E♭	E	F
Open	1 2 3	1 3	2 3	1 2	1

F♯ G♭	G	G♯ A♭	A	A♯ B♭	B
1 2 3	1 3	2 3	1 2 or 3	1	2

C	C♯ D♭	D	D♯ E♭	E	F
Open	1 2 3	1 3	2 3	1 2 or 3	1

F♯ G♭	G	G♯ A♭	A	A♯ B♭	B
2 or 1 2 3	Open or 1 3	2 3	1 2 or 3	1 or 1 2 3	2 or 1 3

C	C♯ D♭	D	D♯ E♭	E	F
Open or 2 3	1 2 or 3	1 or 1 3	2 or 2 3	Open or 1 2	1

F♯ G♭	G	G♯ A♭	A	A♯ B♭	B
2	Open or 1 3	2 3	1 2 or 3	1	2

C	C♯ D♭	D	D♯ E♭	E	F
Open	2 or 1 2	Open or 1	2	Open	1

(When more than one fingering is shown, the first is the most common.)

It is **illegal** to photocopy or reproduce this Trumpet Fingering Chart.

French Horn Harmonic Series

The fundamental pitch of the French Horn is determined by the length of the tube. Its characteristic tone quality is determined not only by the size of the opening in the tube, but also the amount of conical tubing or flare.

Regardless of the length of tubing, a natural overtone series is produced when the air inside the tube is activated through the vibration of the lips. By changing the tension of the lips and air speed, the performer can move higher and lower within the harmonic series, without changing valves. Although the harmonic series is (in theory) endless, the chart below begins with the fundamental and continues through the 16th partial.

The 7th and 11th harmonic (partial) is so flat that it is unusable in the series (note the triangular shape of the note head). For both Horn in F and Horn in B♭ the 5th partial is noticeably flat while the 3rd and 6th harmonics are slightly sharp. *However, different brands of instruments and mouthpieces may produce varying results.*

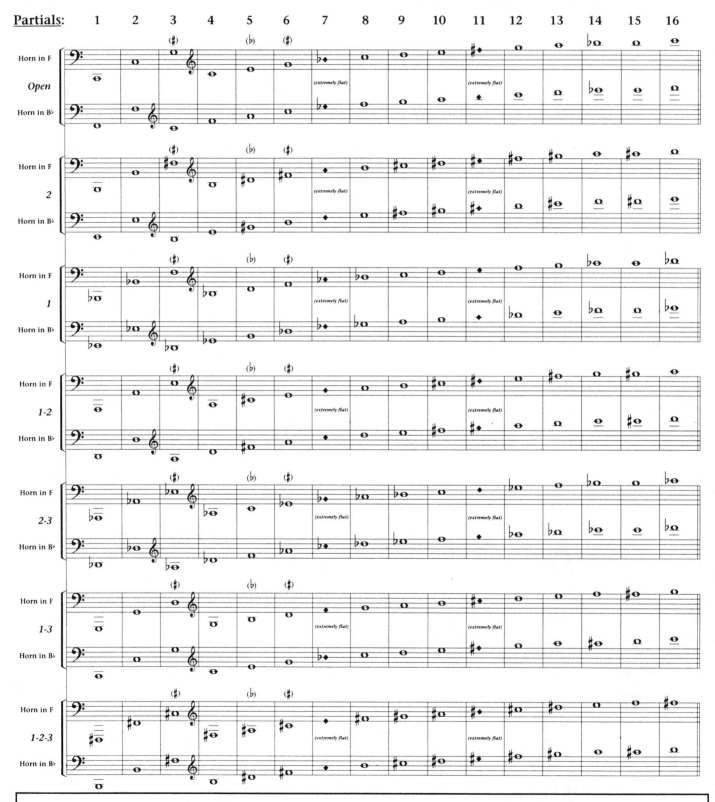

WARNING! It is **illegal** to photocopy or reproduce the French Horn Harmonic Series and Fingering Chart. Individual French Horn Fingering Charts are available for purchase from your favorite music dealer for use with your students. Please refer to the back cover of this manual for further information.
Individual French Horn Fingering Charts: Kjos Edition Number - W33HF

French Horn Fingering Chart

Many players prefer to use the B♭ Horn (trigger) when they reach second line G♯ and continue to use it throughout the upper register.

C	C♯ D♭	D	D♯ E♭	E	F
Open	T 2 3	T 1 2	T 1	T 2	T open

F♯ G♭	G	G♯ A♭	A	A♯ B♭	B
1 2 3	1 3	2 3	1 2	1	2

C	C♯ D♭	D	D♯ E♭	E	F
Open	T 2 3 or 1 2 3	T 1 2 or 1 3	T 1 or 2 3	T 2 or 1 2	T open or 1

F♯ G♭	G	G♯ A♭	A	A♯ B♭	B
2	Open	2 3	1 2	1	2

C	C♯ D♭	D	D♯ E♭	E	F	F♯ G♭
Open or T open	1 2 or T 2 3	1 or T 1 2	2 or T 1	Open or T 2	1 or T open	2

G	G♯ A♭	A	A♯ B♭	B	C
Open	T 2 3 or 2 3	T 1 2 or 1 2	T 1 or 1	T 2 or 2	T open or Open

C♯ D♭	D	D♯ E♭	E	F	F♯ G♭
T 2 3 or 1 2 or 2	T 1 2 or 1 or Open	T 1 or 2	T 2 or Open	T open or 1	T 2 or T 1 2 or 2

G	G♯ A♭	A	A♯ B♭	B	C
T open or T 1 or Open	T 2 3 or T 2 or 2 3	T 1 2 or T open or 1 2	T 1 or 1	T 2 or 2	T open or Open

(When more than one fingering is shown, the first is the most common.)

It is **illegal** to photocopy or reproduce this **French Horn Fingering Chart**.

W33F

Stopped French Horn

The stopped horn technique is usually done on the F side of the horn since stopping the B♭ side of the instrument raises the pitch farther than a half-step.

Stopping the horn is a technique where the right hand is inserted into the bell, blocking off the air completely. As the hand is inserted into the bell, the pitch will become almost a half-step flat. However, when the hand *completely* stops the horn, the pitch is raised a half-step. If done correctly, a C major arpeggio will sound like a C♯ major arpeggio when the horn is stopped:

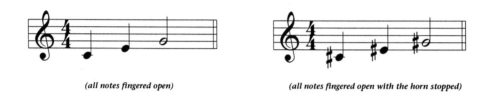

(all notes fingered open)   (all notes fingered open with the horn stopped)

In order to play stopped horn passages, horn players must learn to finger the passage a half-step down from the written pitch (on the F side of the horn) to compensate for the sharpness.

To demonstrate this technique, play the following example the first time with the standard fingerings. Then stop the horn and play the passage again with the indicated fingerings - it should sound the same.

America

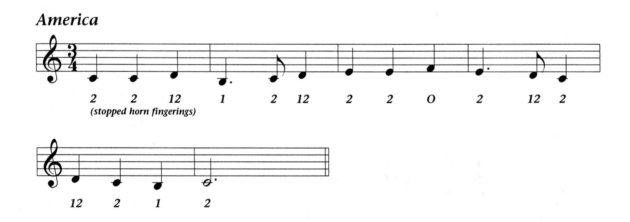

Stopped horn is indicated by the following terms: "stopped" (English), "gestopft" (German), "bouché" (French), and "chiuso" (Italian). In all languages, the sign "+" indicates that the note is stopped and the sign "o" indicates that the note is open.

It is **illegal** to photocopy or reproduce this Stopped French Horn page.

How To Tie A French Horn Valve String

Fig. 1: Tie a small knot at the end of the string.

Insert the thread through the hole in the extension rod from the opposite side.

Fig. 2: Pull the string to set the knot.

Wind the string counterclockwise around one side of the stop arm hub...

Fig. 3: Continue clockwise around the set screw...

Fig. 4 & 5: Finally circle around the stop arm hub.

☆ **Make sure the string passes underneath itself as it completes the figure-eight pattern around the hub and the set screw.**

Run the string through the hole near the end of the extension lever from the inside out.

Fig. 6: With the set screw resting against the stopper, adjust the length of the string so that all the keys are level.

Tighten the set screw.

Finally, form a small loop in the cord with the loose end under-place this over the small set screw and tighten. Cut the excess cord.

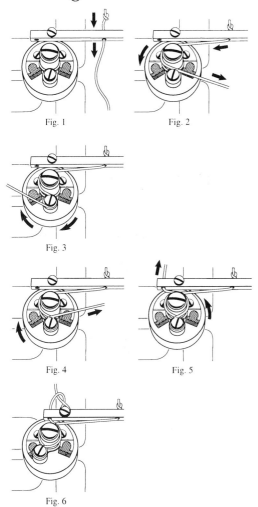

Fig. 1   Fig. 2   Fig. 3   Fig. 4   Fig. 5   Fig. 6

How To Tie A Trombone Trigger String

Fig. 1: Tie a small knot at the end of the string.

Insert the thread through the hole in the extension rod from the opposite side.

Fig. 2: Pull the string to set the knot.

Wind the string clockwise around one side of the stop arm hub...

Fig. 3: Continue counterclockwise around the set screw...

Fig. 4 & 5: Finally circle around the stop arm hub.

☆ **Make sure the string passes underneath itself as it completes the figure-eight pattern around the hub and the set screw.**

Run the string through the hole near the end of the extension lever from the inside out.

Fig. 6: With the set screw resting against the stopper, adjust the length of the string so that all the keys are level.

Tighten the set screw.

Finally, form a small loop in the cord with the loose end under-place this over the small set screw and tighten. Cut the excess cord.

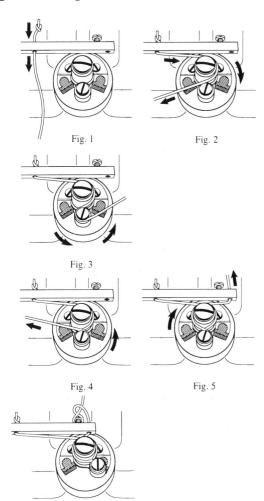

Fig. 1   Fig. 2   Fig. 3   Fig. 4   Fig. 5   Fig. 6

It is **illegal** to photocopy or reproduce this entire page.   W33F

Trombone Harmonic Series

The fundamental pitch of the trombone is determined by the length of the tube. Its characteristic tone quality is determined not only by the size of the opening in the tube, but also the amount of conical tubing or flare.

Regardless of the length of tubing, a natural overtone series is produced when the air inside the tube is activated through the vibration of the lips. By changing the tension of the lips and air speed, the performer can move higher and lower within the harmonic series, without changing the slide positions.

Although the harmonic series is (in theory) endless, the chart below begins with the fundamental and continues through the 12th partial.

The 7th and 11th harmonic (partial) is so flat that it is unusable in the series (note the triangular shape of the note head). *However, different brands of instruments and mouthpieces may produce varying results.*

WARNING! It is **illegal** to photocopy or reproduce the Trombone Harmonic Series and Position Chart. Individual Trombone Position Charts are available for purchase from your favorite music dealer for use with your students. Please refer to the back cover of this manual for further information.

Individual Trombone Position Charts: Kjos Edition Number - W33TB

Trombone Position Chart

Notes on gray background are pedal tones.

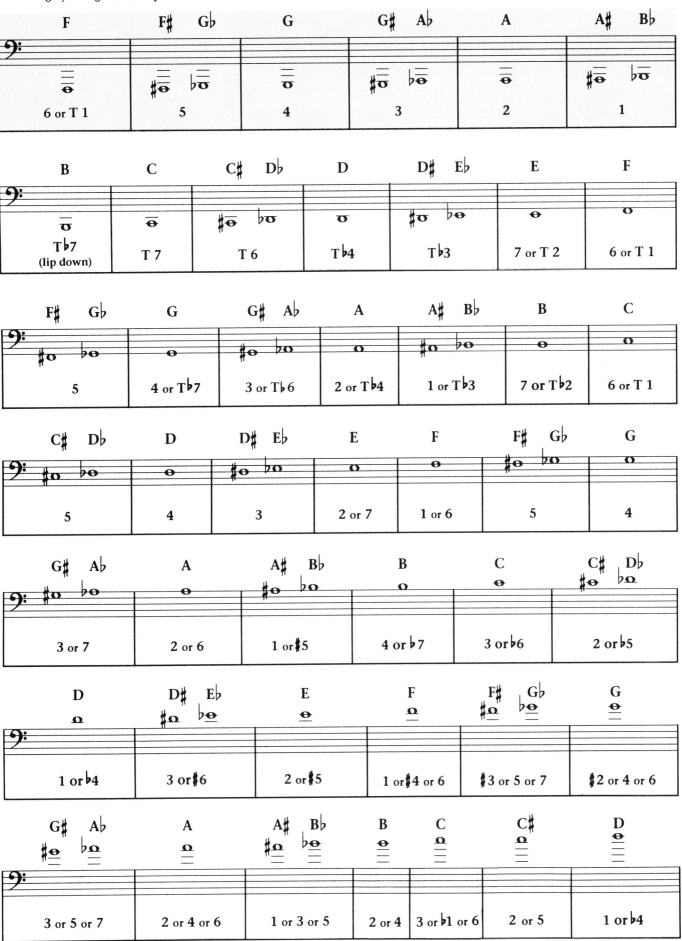

(When more than one position is shown, the first is the most common.)

It is **illegal** to photocopy or reproduce this Trombone Position Chart.

Euphonium B.C. Harmonic Series
Non Compensating & Automatic Compensating

The fundamental pitch of the euphonium is determined by the length of the tube. Its characteristic tone quality is determined not only by the size of the opening in the tube, but also the amount of conical tubing or flare.

Regardless of the length of tubing, a natural overtone series is produced when the air inside the tube is activated through the vibration of the lips. By changing the tension of the lips and air speed, the performer can move higher and lower within the harmonic series, without changing valves.

Although the harmonic series is (in theory) endless, the chart below begins with the fundamental and continues through the 12th partial.

The 7th and 11th harmonic (partial) is so flat that it is unusable in the series (note the triangular shape of the note head). *However, different brands of instruments and mouthpieces may produce varying results.*

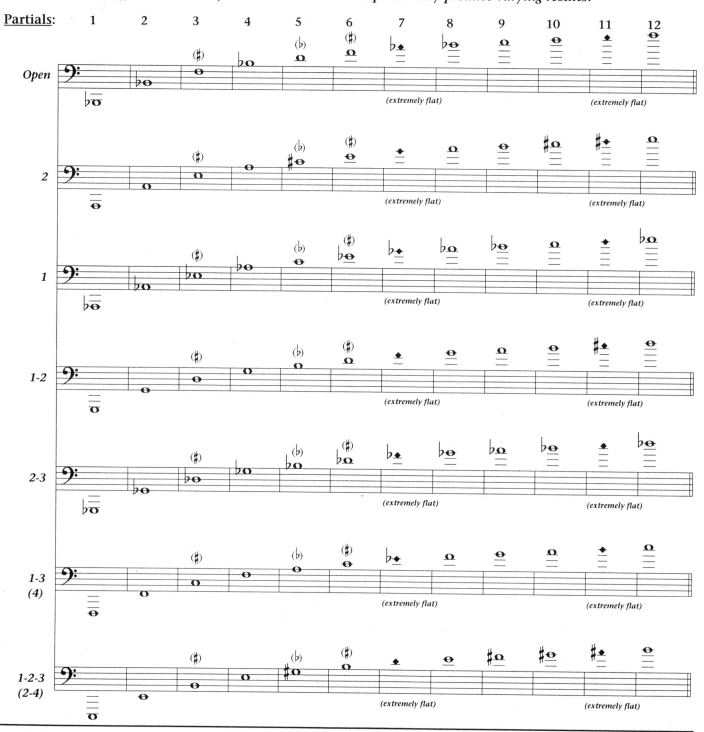

WARNING! It is **illegal** to photocopy or reproduce the Euphonium Harmonic Series and Fingering Chart. Individual Euphonium Fingering Charts are available for purchase from your favorite music dealer for use with your students. Please refer to the back cover of this manual for further information.

Individual Euphonium Fingering Charts: Kjos Edition Numbers

Bass Clef		Treble Clef
W33BCN	Non Compensating	W33TCN
W33BCA	Automatic Compensating	W33TCA

Euphonium B.C. Fingering Chart
Non Compensating

Notes on gray background are pedal tones.

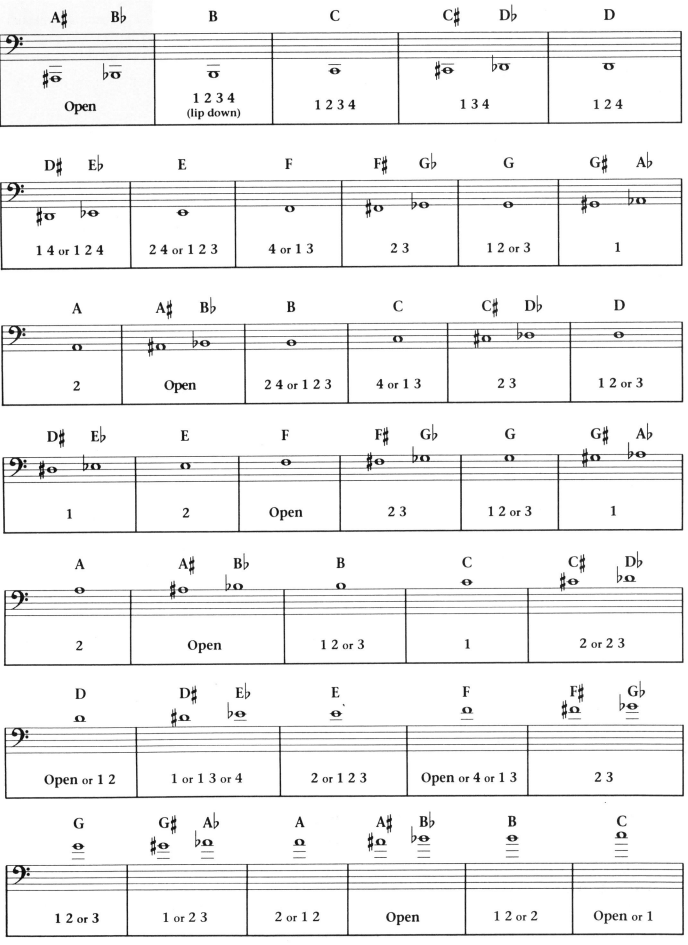

(When more than one fingering is shown, the first is the most common.)

It is **illegal** to photocopy or reproduce this Euphonium Fingering Chart.

W33F

Euphonium T.C. Harmonic Series
Non Compensating & Automatic Compensating

The fundamental pitch of the euphonium is determined by the length of the tube. Its characteristic tone quality is determined not only by the size of the opening in the tube, but also the amount of conical tubing or flare.

Regardless of the length of tubing, a natural overtone series is produced when the air inside the tube is activated through the vibration of the lips. By changing the tension of the lips and air speed, the performer can move higher and lower within the harmonic series, without changing valves.

Although the harmonic series is (in theory) endless, the chart below begins with the fundamental and continues through the 12th partial.

The 7th and 11th harmonic (partial) is so flat that it is unusable in the series (note the triangular shape of the note head). *However, different brands of instruments and mouthpieces may produce varying results.*

WARNING! It is **illegal** to photocopy or reproduce the Euphonium Harmonic Series and Fingering Chart. Individual Euphonium Fingering Charts are available for purchase from your favorite music dealer for use with your students. Please refer to the back cover of this manual for further information.

Individual Euphonium Fingering Charts: Kjos Edition Numbers

Bass Clef		Treble Clef
W33BCN	Non Compensating	W33TCN
W33BCA	Automatic Compensating	W33TCA

Euphonium T.C. Fingering Chart
Non Compensating

Notes on gray background are pedal tones.

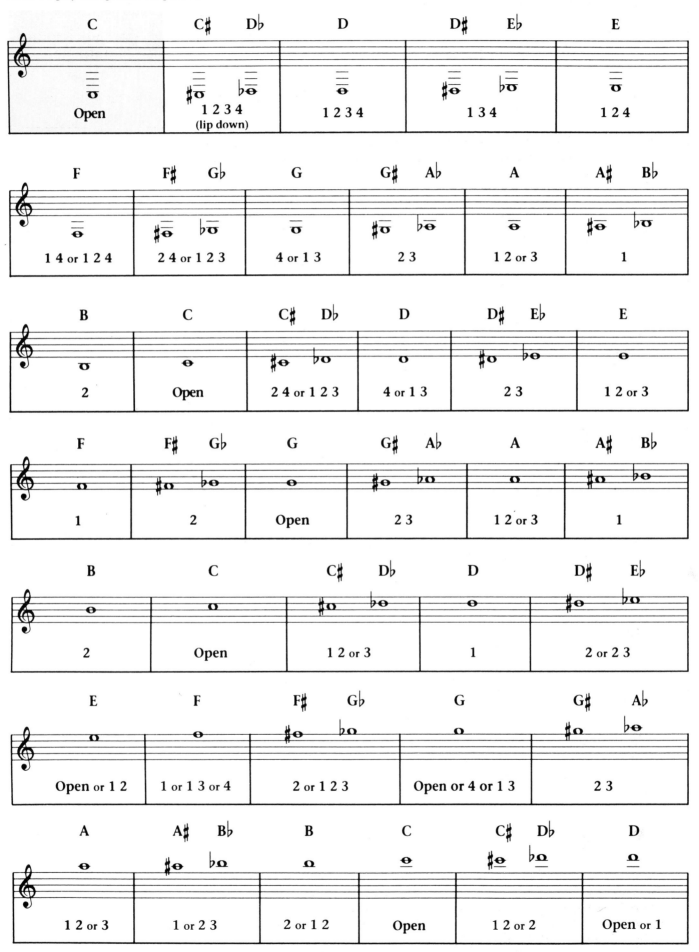

(When more than one fingering is shown, the first is the most common.)

It is **illegal** to photocopy or reproduce this Euphonium Fingering Chart.

W33F

Euphonium T.C. Fingering Chart
Automatic Compensating

Notes on gray background are pedal tones.

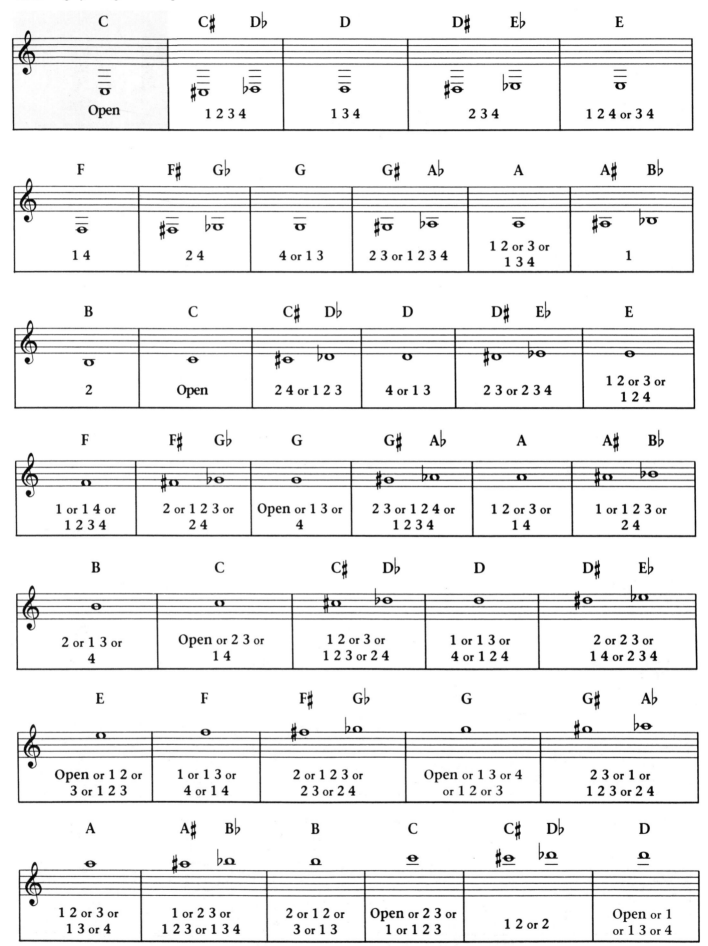

(When more than one fingering is shown, the first is the most common.)

It is **illegal** to photocopy or reproduce this Euphonium Fingering Chart.

Euphonium B.C. Fingering Chart
Automatic Compensating

Notes on gray background are pedal tones.

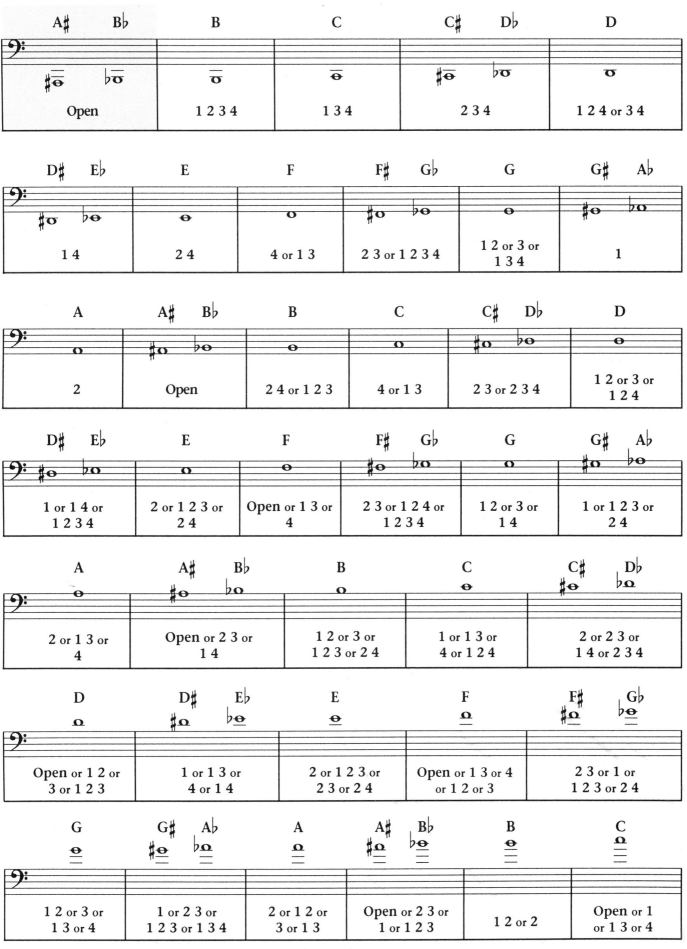

(When more than one fingering is shown, the first is the most common.)

It is **illegal** to photocopy or reproduce this Euphonium Fingering Chart.

W33F

Tuba Harmonic Series

The fundamental pitch of the tuba is determined by the length of the tube. Its characteristic tone quality is determined not only by the size of the opening in the tube, but also the amount of conical tubing or flare.

Regardless of the length of tubing, a natural overtone series is produced when the air inside the tube is activated through the vibration of the lips. By changing the tension of the lips and air speed, the performer can move higher and lower within the harmonic series, without changing valves. Although the harmonic series is (in theory) endless, the chart below begins with the fundamental and continues through the 12th partial.

The 7th and 11th harmonic (partial) is so flat that it is unusable in the series (note the triangular shape of the note head). *However, different brands of instruments and mouthpieces may produce varying results.*

WARNING! It is **illegal** to photocopy or reproduce the Tuba Harmonic Series and Fingering Chart. Individual Tuba Fingering Charts are available for purchase from your favorite music dealer for use with your students. Please refer to the back cover of this manual for further information.

Individual Tuba Fingering Charts: Kjos Edition Number - W33BS

Tuba Fingering Chart

Notes on gray background are pedal tones

	A# Bb	B	C	C# Db	D	D# Eb	E	F
BB♭ Tuba	Open	* (2 3)	1 2 3 4↓ or 1 2 or 3	1 3 4 or 1	2 3 4 or 2	1 2 4 or 1 4↓ or Open	2 4 or 1 2 3↓	4 or 1 3↓
CC Tuba	1	2	Open	* (2 3)	1 2 3 4↓ or 1 2↑ or 3	1 3 4↓ or 1	2 3 4 or 2	1 2 4 or 1 4↓ or Open
**E♭ Tuba	4 or 1 3	2 3	1 2 or 3	1	2	Open	* (2 3)	1 2 3 4↓ or 1 2 or 3

	F# Gb	G	G# Ab	A	A# Bb	B	C	C# Db
BB♭ Tuba	2 3	1 2 or 3	1	2	Open	2 4 or 1 2 3↓	4 or 1 3↓	2 3
CC Tuba	2 4 or 1 2 3↓	4 or 1 3↓	2 3	1 2 or 3	1	2	Open	2 4 or 1 2 3↓
**E♭ Tuba	1 3 4↓ or 1	2 3 4 or 2	1 2 4 or 1 4↓ or Open	2 4 or 1 2 3↓	4 or 1 3↓	2 3	1 2 or 3	1

	D	D# Eb	E	F	F# Gb	G	G# Ab	A
BB♭ Tuba	1 2 or 3	1	2	Open or 1 3↓ or 4	2 3	1 2 or 3	1	2
CC Tuba	4 or 1 3↓	2 3	1 2 or 3	1	2	Open or 1 3↓	2 3	1 2 or 3
**E♭ Tuba	2	Open	2 4 or 1 2 3↓	4 or 1 3↓	2 3	1 2 or 3	1	2

	A# Bb	B	C	C# Db	D	D# Eb	E	F
BB♭ Tuba	Open or 2 3	1 2↑ or 3 or 2 4	1↑ or 1 3↓ or 4	2 or 2 3	Open or 1 2↓ or 3	1↓ or 1 3↑	2 or 2 3↑	Open or 1 2↑ or 3↑
CC Tuba	1	2	Open or 2 3	1 2↑ or 3 or 2 4	1↑ or 1 3↓ or 4	2 or 2 3	Open or 1 2↓ or 3	1↓ or 1 3↑
**E♭ Tuba	Open or 1 3↓	2 3	1 2 or 3	1 or 1 2 3	2 or 1 3	Open or 2 3	1 2 or 3	1 or 13

	F# Gb	G	G# Ab	A	A# Bb	B	C	C# Db
BB♭ Tuba	2 3 or 1↑	1 2 or 3 or 2↑	1 or Open or 2 3 or 2 4	2 or 1 2 or 1 3	Open or 2 3↑ or 1	1 2 or 3 or 2 4	1↑ or Open or 1 3 or 4↑	2 or 2 3
CC Tuba	2 or 2 3↑	Open or 1 2↑ or 3↑	2 3 or 1↑	1 2 or 3 or 2↑	1 or Open or 2 3 or 2 4	2 or 1 2 or 1 3	Open or 2 3↑ or 1	1 2 or 3 or 2 4
**E♭ Tuba	2 or 2 3	Open or 1 2 or 3	1 or 1 3	2	Open or 1 2↑	2 3 or 1↑	1 2 or 3 or 2↑	1 or Open or 2 3 or 2 4

	D	D# Eb	E	F	F# Gb	G	G# Ab	A	A# Bb
BB♭ Tuba	Open or 1 2 or 1 2 3 or 3	1 or 1 3	2 or 2 3	Open or 1 2	2 3 or 1	1 2 or 2	1 or Open or 2 3 or 2 4	2 or 1 2 or 1 3	Open or 2 3 or 1
CC Tuba	1↑ or Open or 1 3↓ or 4↑	2 or 2 3	Open or 1 2 or 1 2 3 or 3	1 or 1 3	2 or 2 3	Open or 1 2	2 3 or 1	1 2 or 2	1 or Open or 2 3 or 2 4
**E♭ Tuba	2 or 1 2 or 1 3	Open or 2 3 or 1	1 2 or 3 or 2 4	1 or 1 3↓ or Open	2 or 2 3	1 2 3 or 3 or Open or 1 2	1 or 1 3	2 or 2 3	Open or 1 2

(When more than one fingering is shown, the first is the most common.)
*Not readily playable on 4 valve Tuba.   **Non Compensating.   ↓ = Lower pitch   ↑ = Raise pitch

W33F   Musical instruments on the cover provided courtesy of the G. Leblanc Corporation, Kenosha, Wisconsin, U.S.A.

A Brief Guide to Ornamentation (Treble Clef)

Ornamentation is the practice of adding notes to a melodic line. Basically, an ornament is a set of auxiliary notes associated with a main note. When working out an ornament, it is important to consider the composer's intent and the performance practice of the era in which the music was written. Also take into account the following:

- the time signature of the passage

- the key signature of the passage and any accidentals indicated in the ornament's notation

- the number of beats or subdivisions that the ornament must fill and how the rhythm should be subdivided

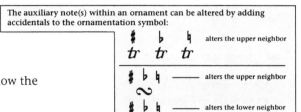

Grace Notes

Grace notes appear as small notes which have no rhythmic value of their own. They take their duration from the previous or following beat.

Grace notes usually appear as small eighth-notes or a small eighth-note with a cross stroke through the stem and flag.

In groups of two or three they appear as 16th notes and in groups of four or more they are often written as 32nd notes.

Baroque (1600-1750) and Classical (1750-1830) era grace notes are always played on the beat and usually take half the value of the note that follows it (even though it appears as a small eighth-note). If the grace note precedes a dotted note it takes two-thirds of the main note's value.

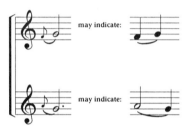

Since the Romantic era (1830-1900), grace notes precede the beat of the main note.

Mordent

Mordents are played on the beat as rapidly as possible. This creates a rhythmic accent as well as a short-lived dissonance.

Baroque era mordents consist of playing the main note followed quickly by its <u>lower</u> neighbor in the key and returning to the main note.

A mordent symbol without the line is played with the main note followed quickly by its <u>upper</u> neighbor in the key and returning to the main note.

Turns

Turns are performed by playing the upper neighbor in the key, the main note, the lower neighbor in the key, and finally the main note.

When the turn is written over the main note, the ornament begins on the beat starting with the upper neighbor in the key.

When the turn is written after the main note, the main note is played before the ornament.

Trills

Trills are performed as rapid repetitions of a main note and its upper neighbor in the key. Most trills which occur at cadence points finish with a "turned ending" (termination) whether it is indicated or not. The number of repetitions in a trill will depend on the value of the main note, the tempo of the passage, and the skill and artistic sensibility of the performer.

From the Romantic era to the present:
- start the trill on the beat
- begin the trill on the main note
- no termination unless notated
- may start slowly and increase in speed

In the Baroque and Classical eras:
- start the trill on the beat • begin the trill on the auxiliary (upper) note • terminations may or may not be indicated
- short trills require a minimum of two repetitions

It is **illegal** to photocopy or reproduce this Guide to Ornamentation.

W33F

A Brief Guide to Ornamentation (Bass Clef)

Ornamentation is the practice of adding notes to a melodic line. Basically, an ornament is a set of auxiliary notes associated with a main note. When working out an ornament, it is important to consider the composer's intent and the performance practice of the era in which the music was written. Also take into account the following:

- the time signature of the passage

- the key signature of the passage and any accidentals indicated in the ornament's notation

- the number of beats or subdivisions that the ornament must fill and how the rhythm should be subdivided

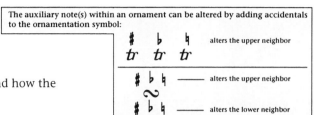

Grace Notes

Grace notes appear as small notes which have no rhythmic value of their own. They take their duration from the previous or following beat.

Grace notes usually appear as small eighth-notes or a small eighth-note with a cross stroke through the stem and flag.

In groups of two or three they appear as 16th notes and in groups of four or more they are often written as 32nd notes.

Baroque (1600-1750) and Classical (1750-1830) era grace notes are always played on the beat and usually take half the value of the note that follows it (even though it appears as a small eighth-note). If the grace note precedes a dotted note it takes two-thirds of the main note's value.

Since the Romantic era (1830-1900), grace notes precede the beat of the main note.

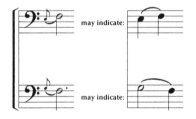

Mordent

Mordents are played on the beat as rapidly as possible. This creates a rhythmic accent as well as a short-lived dissonance.

Baroque era mordents consist of playing the main note followed quickly by its lower neighbor in the key and returning to the main note.

A mordent symbol without the line is played with the main note followed quickly by its upper neighbor in the key and returning to the main note.

Turns

Turns are performed by playing the upper neighbor in the key, the main note, the lower neighbor in the key, and finally the main note.

When the turn is written over the main note, the ornament begins on the beat starting with the upper neighbor in the key.

When the turn is written after the main note, the main note is played before the ornament.

Trills

Trills are performed as rapid repetitions of a main note and its upper neighbor in the key. Most trills which occur at cadence points finish with a "turned ending" (termination) whether it is indicated or not. The number of repetitions in a trill will depend on the value of the main note, the tempo of the passage, and the skill and artistic sensibility of the performer.

From the Romantic era to the present:
- start the trill on the beat
- begin the trill on the main note
- no termination unless notated
- may start slowly and increase in speed

In the Baroque and Classical eras:
- start the trill on the beat • begin the trill on the auxiliary (upper) note • terminations may or may not be indicated
- short trills require a minimum of two repetitions

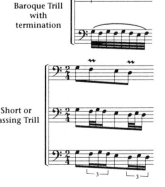

It is **illegal** to photocopy or reproduce this Guide to Ornamentation.

Keyboard Percussion Ranges

The following diagrams outline the full range of each instrument. The lowest and highest notes are indicated as well as the location of written middle C. **Please note that instrument size and range may vary according to the manufacturer.**

Orchestra Bells or Glockenspiel (sounds two octaves higher than notated)

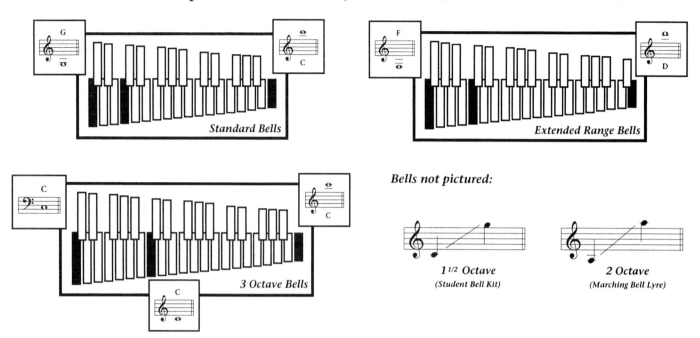

Bells not pictured:

1 1/2 Octave
(Student Bell Kit)

2 Octave
(Marching Bell Lyre)

Crotales (sounds two octaves higher than notated)

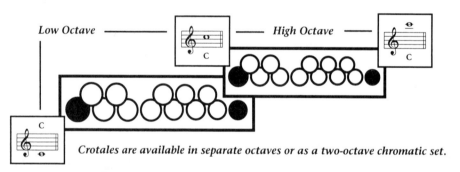

Crotales are available in separate octaves or as a two-octave chromatic set.

Xylophone (sounds one octave higher than notated)

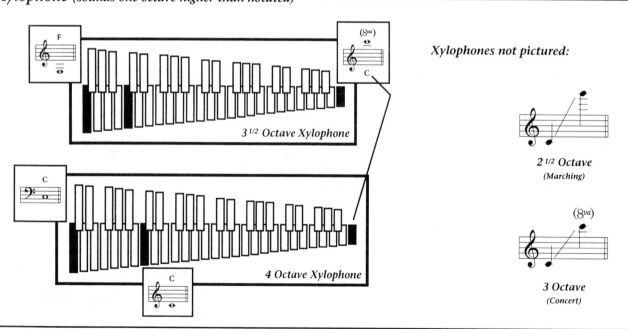

Xylophones not pictured:

2 1/2 Octave
(Marching)

3 Octave
(Concert)

WARNING! It is **illegal** to photocopy or reproduce the Percussion Diagram and Drum Rudiment Charts. Individual Percussion Diagram and Drum Rudiment Charts are available for purchase from your favorite music dealer for use with your students. Please refer to the back cover of this manual for further information.
Individual Percussion Diagram and Drum Rudiments Charts
Kjos Edition Number - W33PR

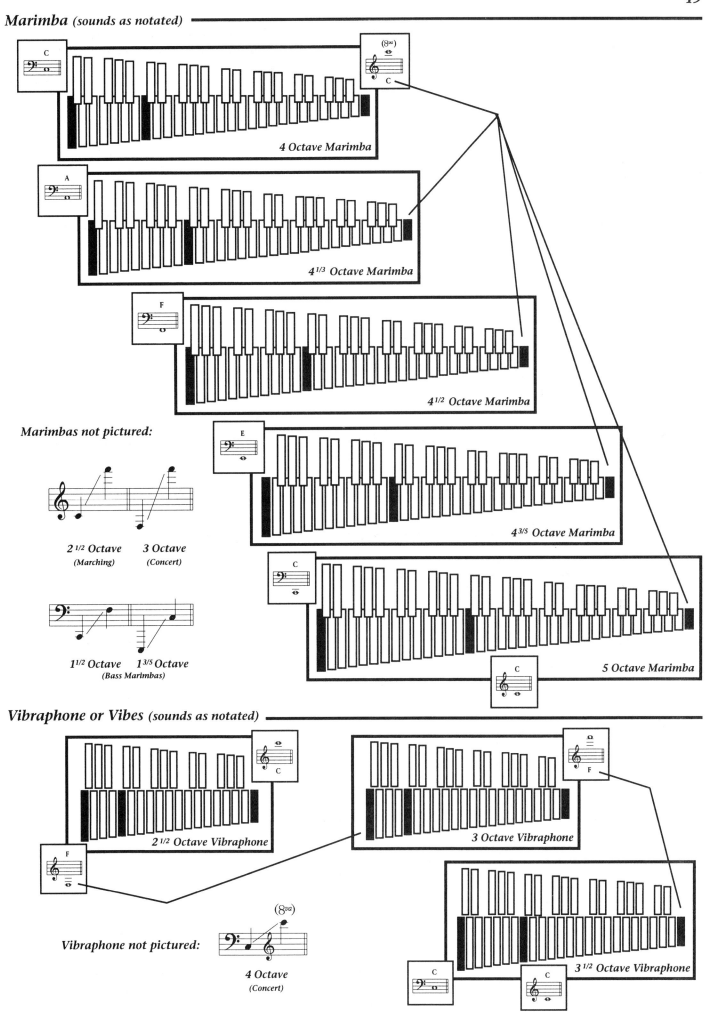

Marimba (sounds as notated)

4 Octave Marimba

4 1/3 Octave Marimba

4 1/2 Octave Marimba

Marimbas not pictured:

2 1/2 Octave (Marching) 3 Octave (Concert)

1 1/2 Octave 1 3/5 Octave (Bass Marimbas)

4 3/5 Octave Marimba

5 Octave Marimba

Vibraphone or Vibes (sounds as notated)

2 1/2 Octave Vibraphone

3 Octave Vibraphone

Vibraphone not pictured:

4 Octave (Concert)

3 1/2 Octave Vibraphone

It is **illegal** to photocopy or reproduce these Keyboard Percussion Diagrams.

Keyboard Percussion Ranges (Cont.)

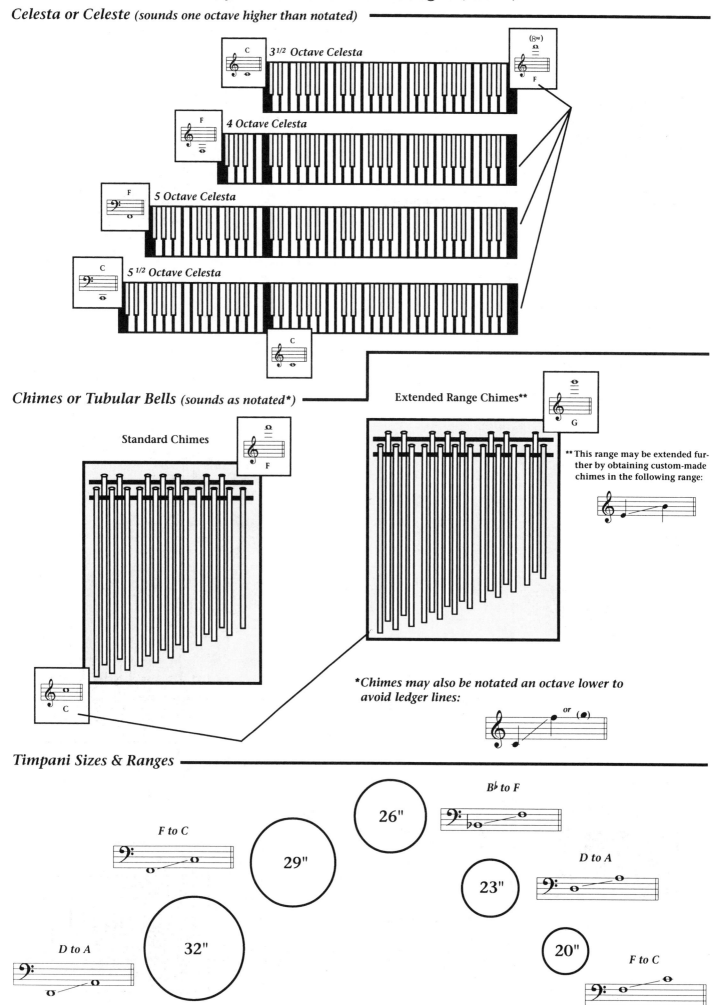

Celesta or Celeste (sounds one octave higher than notated)

3 1/2 Octave Celesta

4 Octave Celesta

5 Octave Celesta

5 1/2 Octave Celesta

Chimes or Tubular Bells (sounds as notated*)

Standard Chimes

Extended Range Chimes**

** This range may be extended further by obtaining custom-made chimes in the following range:

*Chimes may also be notated an octave lower to avoid ledger lines:

Timpani Sizes & Ranges

26" Bb to F

F to C 29"

23" D to A

32"

D to A 20" F to C

It is **illegal** to photocopy or reproduce these Keyboard Percussion and Timpani Diagrams.

Major Scale & Arpeggio Diagrams

The following diagrams outline one octave scales and arpeggios in all the 12 major key signatures. Note the (▲) shows the position of middle C.

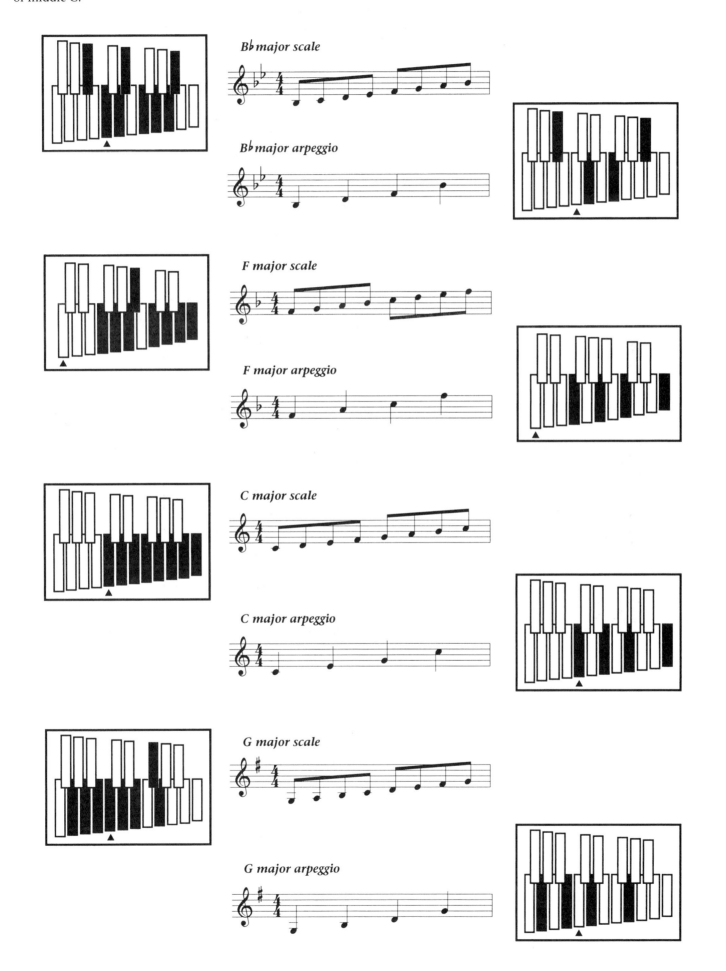

It is **illegal** to photocopy or reproduce these Major Scale and Arpeggio Diagrams.

W33F

Major Scale & Arpeggio Diagrams (Cont.)

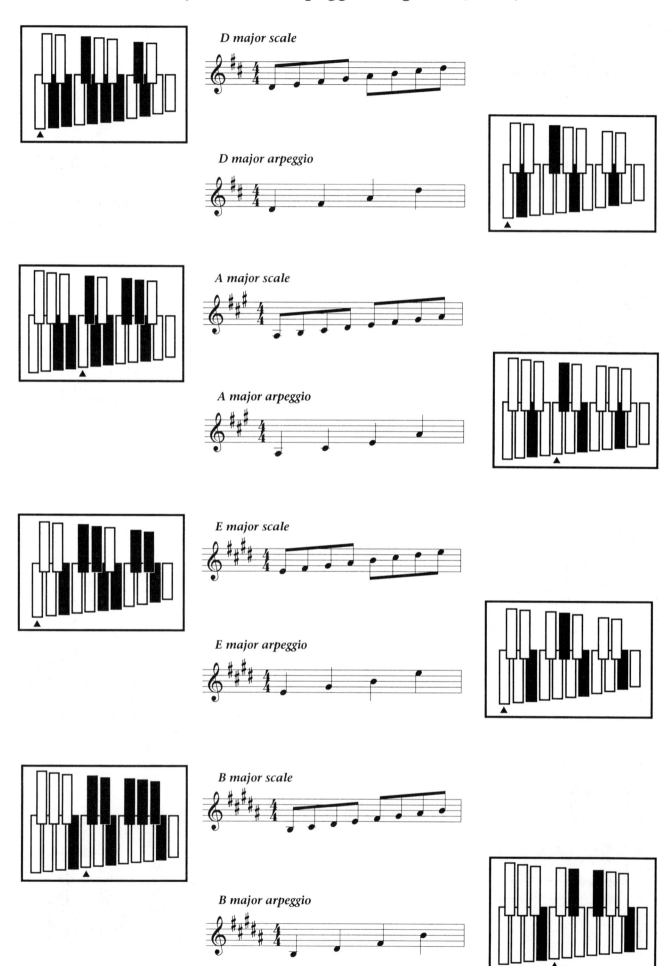

It is **illegal** to photocopy or reproduce these Major Scale and Arpeggio Diagrams.

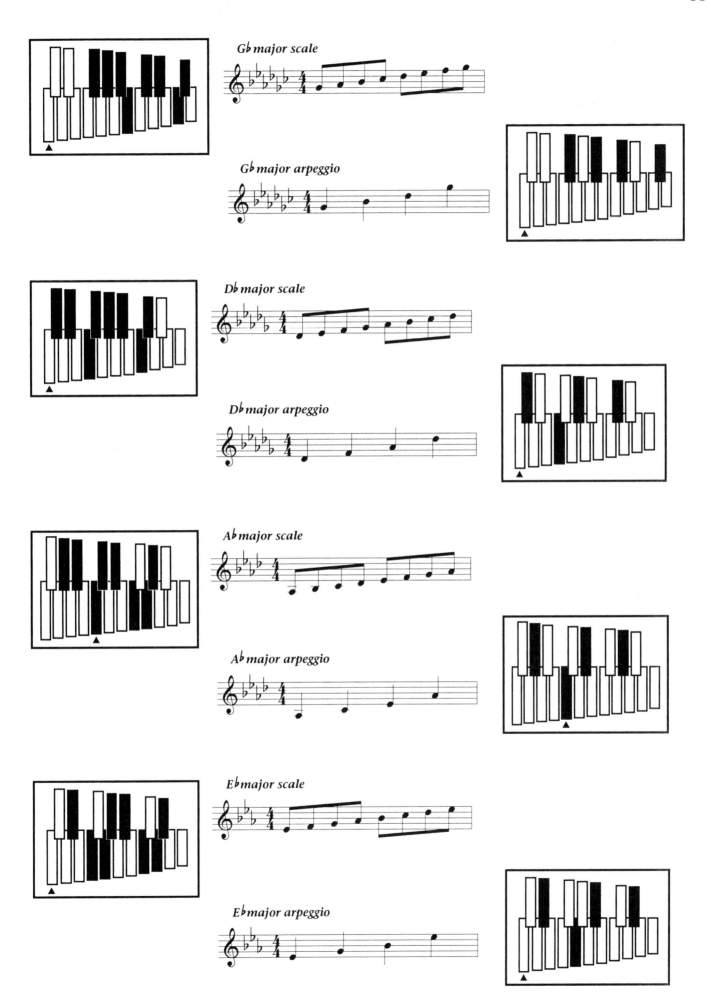

G♭ major scale

G♭ major arpeggio

D♭ major scale

D♭ major arpeggio

A♭ major scale

A♭ major arpeggio

E♭ major scale

E♭ major arpeggio

It is **illegal** to photocopy or reproduce these Major Scale and Arpeggio Diagrams.

Standard Drum Rudiments <small>(as adopted by the Percussive Arts Society)</small>

The following rudiments may be played at a set tempo or "Open - Close - Open" by starting at a slow tempo, playing with a gradual accelerando followed by a gradual ritard back to the starting tempo. **The provided counting system is meant to serve only as a guide** - *any* counting system may be substituted.

Single Stroke Rolls

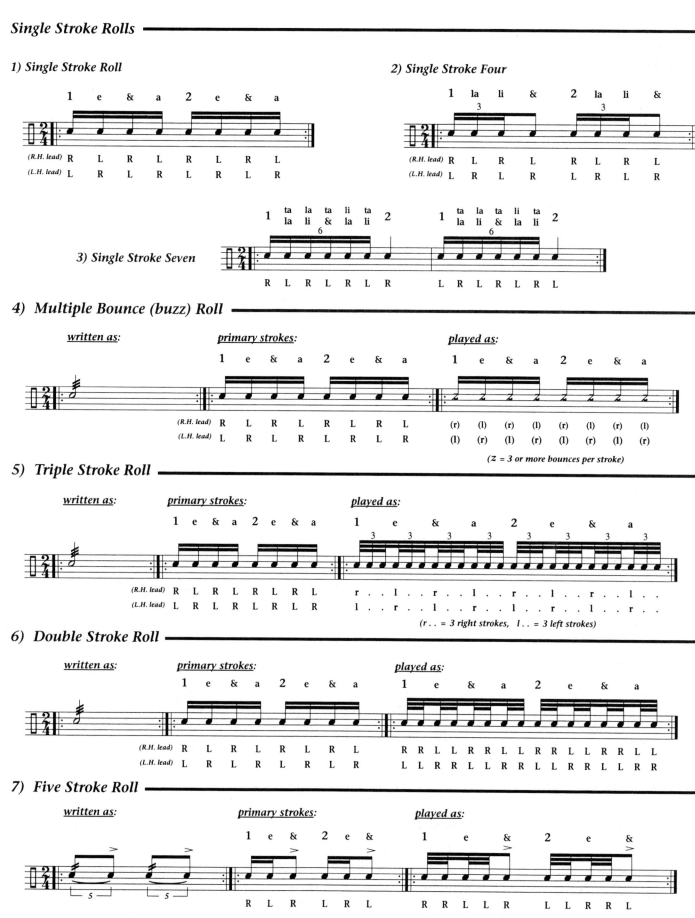

1) Single Stroke Roll

2) Single Stroke Four

3) Single Stroke Seven

4) Multiple Bounce (buzz) Roll

5) Triple Stroke Roll

6) Double Stroke Roll

7) Five Stroke Roll

It is **illegal** to photocopy or reproduce these Drum Rudiments.

8) Six Stroke Roll

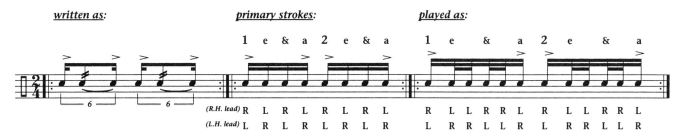

9) Seven Stroke Rolls

• Duple Pulse

• Triple Pulse

10) Nine Stroke Roll

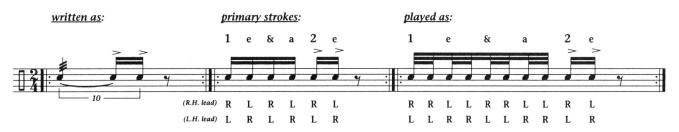

11) Ten Stroke Roll

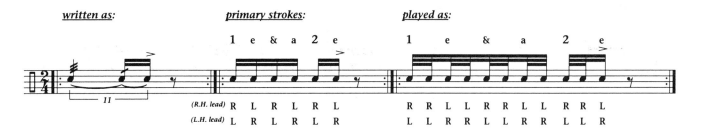

12) Eleven Stroke Roll

It is **illegal** to photocopy or reproduce these Drum Rudiments.

Standard Drum Rudiments (Cont.)

13) Thirteen Stroke Roll

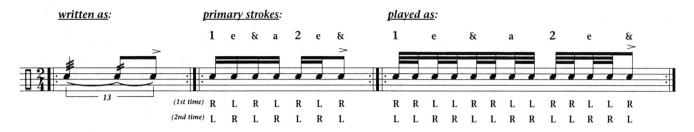

14) Fifteen Stroke Roll

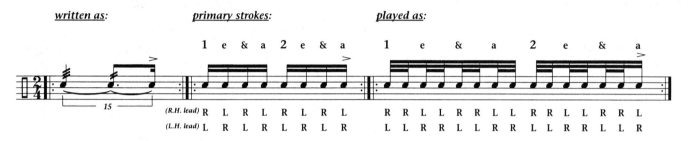

15) Seventeen Stroke Roll

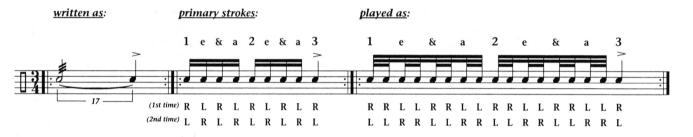

Diddle Rudiments

16) Single Paradiddle

17) Double Paradiddle

18) Triple Paradiddle

19) Single Paradiddle-Diddle

Flam Rudiments

20) Flam

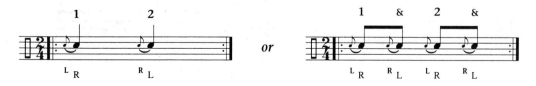

It is **illegal** to photocopy or reproduce these Drum Rudiments.

Flam Rudiments (cont.)

21) Flam Accent

22) Flam Tap

23) Flamacue
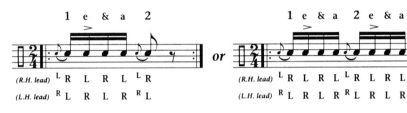

or

24) Flam Paradiddle

25) Single Flammed Mill

26) Flam Paradiddle-Diddle

27) Pataflafla

28) Swiss Army Triplet

29) Inverted Flam Tap

30) Flam Drag

Drag Rudiments

31) Drag

32) Single Drag Tap
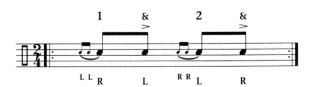

It is **illegal** to photocopy or reproduce these Drum Rudiments.

Standard Drum Rudiments (Cont.)

Drag Rudiments (cont.)

33) Double Drag Tap

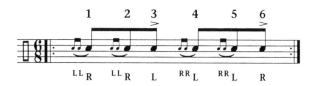

34) Lesson 25

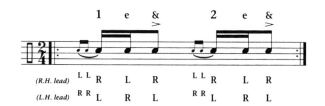

35) Single Dragadiddle

36) Drag Paradiddle #1

37) Drag Paradiddle #2

38) Single Ratamacue

39) Double Ratamacue

40) Triple Ratamacue

A Brief Background on Drum Rudiments (conductor's reference only)

Drum rudiments are the fundamentals of drumming. These rhythmic patterns consist of single, double, and combination beats on the drum. Rudimental historian, George Carroll, in a 1993 seminar presented at the Percussive Arts Society International Convention, stated that rudiments should "be memorized and practiced until they become reflexes, playable accurately at a high rate of speed." Notations of drum rudiments can be traced back to *Orchesographie*, written by Thoinot Arbeau in 1588. The first person to use the term *rudiment* was supposedly Charles Stewart Ashworth in his 1812 text, *A New Useful and Complete System of Drum Beating*. In 1933, the National Association of Rudimental Drummers established and disseminated *The 26 Standard Drum Rudiments*, which in 1985, was revised by the Percussive Arts Society. The PAS list today includes the standard 26 NARD rudiments along with 14 others, making a total of 40 drum rudiments that are presented in this resource.

It is **illegal** to photocopy or reproduce these Drum Rudiments.

Acknowledgments

The authors wish to thank the many people who assisted directly and indirectly in the preparation of this book.

- The entire staff at the **Neil A. Kjos Music Company** for their encouragement and support of music education.

- **Don Minaglia,** for his perseverance and dedication to this project from start to finish.

- Musicians contributing to the woodwind books:

  Melinda Schwieg, Cindy Paxton, and **Dr. Mary Karen Clardy** - flute
  Tracey Jones, Mike Rowden, and **Dr. James Hobbs** - oboe
  Kent Moore, Jenny Mann and **Scott Walzel** - bassoon
  Ricky J. Reeves and **Dr. James Gillespie** - clarinet
  Darin Burris, Jeff Bair and **Greg Ball** - saxophone

- Musicians contributing to the brass books:

  Bert Truax, Alex Dvorak, and **Mary Benner** - trumpet
  Timothy Stevens - horn
  John Kitzman, Keith Meek and **Brian Merrill** - trombone
  Brian Bowman and **John Rider** - euphonium
  Don Little and **John Rider** - tuba

- Duncanville I.S.D., for a great place to teach band.

- To our students, both past and present, who always ask us for fingerings.

To my wife and daughter, Leslie and Lauren King.

To my wife and son, Rebecca and Joseph Williams.